Who Will Save
Our Schools?

CORWIN
PRESS

The Corwin Press logo—a raven striding across an open book—represents the happy union of courage and learning. We are a professional-level publisher of books and journals for K-12 educators, and we are committed to creating and providing resources that embody these qualities. Corwin's motto is "Success for All Learners."

Who Will Save Our Schools?

Teachers as Constructivist Leaders

Linda Lambert
Michelle Collay
Mary E. Dietz
Karen Kent
Anna Ershler Richert

CORWIN PRESS, INC.
A Sage Publications Company
Thousand Oaks, California

For information address:

Corwin Press, Inc.
A Sage Publications Company
2455 Teller Road
Thousand Oaks, California 91320
E-mail: order@corwin.sagepub.com

SAGE Publications Ltd.
6 Bonhill Street
London EC2A 4PU
United Kingdom

SAGE Publications India Pvt. Ltd.
M-32 Market
Greater Kailash I
New Delhi 110 048 India

Printed in the United States of America

Library of Congress Cataloging-in-Publication Data

Who will save our schools? : teachers as constructivist leaders /
    authors, Linda Lambert . . . [et al.].
        p.   cm.
    Includes bibliographical references and index.
    ISBN 0-8039-6462-5 (acid-free paper). — ISBN 0-8039-6463-3 (pbk.:
acid-free paper)
    1. Teacher participation in administration—United States.
    2. Educational leadership—United States. 3. Educational change—
United States. I. Lambert, Linda, 1939–
LB2806.45.W56 1996
371.2—dc20   96-35665

97 98 99 00 01 02 03 10 9 8 7 6 5 4 3 2 1

Acquiring Editor: Alice G. Foster
Editorial Assistant: Nicole Fountain
Production Editor: Sherrise Purdum
Production Assistant: Karen Wiley
Copy Editor: Elizabeth Yoder
Typesetter/Designer: Christina Hill
Cover Designer: Marcia R. Finlayson

Contents

Foreword

WHO WILL SAVE OUR SCHOOLS? PROVOKES ME. Like so many teachers who see our schools criticized in the media and our students settle for mediocrity, I read the literature hoping to find some strategy that will fix both my school and my students. It is a literature of complaint, blame, and even humor. While experts continue to analyze and discuss the problems, and teachers continue to hope for easy solutions, it becomes clear that the nation's schools are not going to change until the people who work in them change. That we teachers are the solution to our own problems is encouraging. This book suggests that schools will change when teachers become constructivist leaders. Teachers becoming leaders in school change is not an idea that will sit well with either teachers or school administrators. We have too many models of powerless teachers in poorly managed schools to fall back on.

Because Americans are an optimistic people and because we have all been in school, there is no lack of advice on how to fix our schools. If teachers would only . . . and when students . . . then our schools. . . . It seems everyone has advice for us. A colleague tells the story of three time travelers from 1896. The carpenter arrives at a construction site and is transfixed at the change of tools and techniques now used in the trade. The doctor observes a bypass operation and is speechless at the equipment and skill of the surgeon. In the classroom, the teacher listens for a moment and then walks to the board, picks up a piece of chalk, and begins to lecture. Even as I laugh, I find myself trying to explain that, yes, it might be true, but . . . Walt Kelly's Pogo had it right: We've met the enemy, and he is us.

Change in school takes a long time. To be sure, the changes in society are all too clearly mirrored in the classrooms of America; yet seventh-grade classes today look amazingly like my seventh-grade class 40 years ago. Biology still precedes chemistry today, and only college-bound students confront physics just as they have been doing for years. When Sputnik's beeps sent us all into the science labs, the delivery system for the new curriculum was not questioned. If more science is needed, then teach more science. If Johnny can't read, then teach reading. Shifting curriculum demands were easily adjustable problems, but few people ever questioned that the schools would provide the necessary changes. The efficiency of top-down administration was obvious and unquestioned. Teachers, once they were told what to do, would do it. Now, with louder cries for changes in curriculum and criticisms about the way schools are managed, the school's ability to deliver curriculum is being questioned.

Public debate over school funding and school choice has caused the very nature of public schooling to be examined. Top-down, state-mandated reforms have long been the standard solution to problems in education; and that hierarchical system is one of the most obvious targets of school critics. It is ironic that we all know public school teachers who vote for voucher plans. Those votes are one way dissatisfied teachers voice their criticisms of a system that no longer listens to their experience or their firsthand understanding of needed changes. *Who Will Save Our Schools?* proposes that teachers become proactive in their schools. Schools must become more than associations of isolated classrooms. An ecological web links students, community, and teachers. Solutions to school problems will be discovered by groups of teachers, students, and community members working in concert, school by school.

Who Will Save Our Schools? speaks to all of us who are interested in school reform. Considering the questions about schooling and reflecting on the nature of the debates about school change, the authors focus on the classroom teacher. The voices of teachers weave through the book. A faculty meeting begins as an outlet for frustration about students and homework when a teacher challenges the old, set patterns of assumptions: "What if we set those ideas aside and really found out what is going on?" When teachers are learners too, the business of school shifts from a place where only students come to be taught to a place where people come to learn. Karen Kent and Anna Richert's work focuses directly on teacher researchers and student teachers and recognizes how vital adult learning is to teaching. Linda Lambert and Michelle Collay have worked extensively with teachers focusing on organizational change, and Mary Dietz concentrates on communities' building capacity for constructivist models of teaching and learning.

Learning and leadership are linked ideas: "The idea that teachers learn in collaboration with others is central to the model of constructivist teacher learning." And if teachers learn in collaboration with others, then we know how students learn. For too long schools have been characterized by fragmentation. Schools have organized themselves into easily identifiable parts reflecting a highly mechanized worldview. Bells ring; Spanish is divided into 1, 2, and 3 parts; and students take math. But as we reconsider the way the world seems to work, we find evidence that supports an ecological, whole system view. Fritjof Capra and others at the Center for Ecoliteracy in Berkeley are describing an integrated world that demonstrates ecological principles at play. Cooperation among organisms is more understandable than survival of the fittest. How can schools continue to justify failure as a piece of what we are about? In this ecological system, leadership is contextual and is based on knowledge and expertise, not on a job description. We have to look at how our schools are organized and what consequences follow from that organization. Whole school systems need to be reviewed and revised. "That's not my job description" never did ring true.

Teachers are forewarned that the ideas in *Who Will Save Our Schools?* are disturbing. The familiar pattern of school organization and our acceptance of business as usual are being challenged. Constructivist teachers working in schools as active learning communities will confront failing programs. Success is ours to take. In this story there are no villains to blame and no heroes to save us; there are no templates to lay over our schools, no facile formulas to implement Monday morning. What is offered us instead are hard, tough questions about what we do and why we do it. Here are the reflections of serious, thoughtful teachers who have insights about their work and about how our schools can survive and prosper using models of learning and teaching that more accurately reflect the nature of learning and of the world. What can be more provocative than the opportunity to save our schools?

> *Tom Abbey*
> Teacher, Humanities 7/8 and 11/12
> Calistoga Junior Senior High School
> Calistoga, CA 94515

Preface

THIS BOOK IS FOR TEACHERS—AND THOSE WHO care about teaching and learning. It is also about reform and for those who care about the future of our children and our society. We link those two words, *teachers* and *reform,* by proposing that teachers, as leaders, must take primary responsibility for the reform of the profession of teaching and the reform of our schools. Why teachers? Why now?

The Predictable Failure of Reform

During the past several decades, the education system in the United States has been in a self-proclaimed state of reform. This continuous state of reform has represented a major issue for teachers, suggesting how they should teach, how they should group students, and how they should design curriculum. Major responsibility for these reforms has been assumed by a myriad of people, groups, and initiatives, including federal initiatives (e.g., Titles I-4C, Goals 2000), Council of Governors, state legislatures, "blue ribbon" commissions on educational reform, state departments of education, state credentialing and licensure commissions, professional association task forces, the university research and writing community, business roundtables, county and regional task forces, foundation initiatives, and district strategic plans. Each of these contenders has undertaken the noble effort; each has fallen short of success.

The road to reform has been paved with various philosophies and theories, as well as navigated by educators, policymakers, and politicians. During this reform process, we have struggled with traditionalism, efficiency, behaviorism, and effectiveness. We have seen a resurgence of Dewey's ideas from the early Progressive movement that has shaped many of the reform agendas since the 1960s: self-directed learners, the role of experience and authentic work, creativity and group interaction, more flexible and less structured time, democratic approaches, problem solving and critical thought, choice and options, respect for relevance. Yet as Linda Darling-Hammond (1993) pointed out, these reforms have failed to match expectations or have arisen in isolated islands of practice. At the top of the list of causes is "a failure of reformers, policymakers, and communities to address the capacity of schools and the teaching profession to implement the reforms" (quoted in Futrell, 1994, p. 120).

The New Road Ahead

The sense of urgency to succeed with reform is heightened by the continuing drop in confidence in and the paradoxical rise in expectations for public education, the demands of a global economy for knowledge and skill, the concerns about violence and growth of prisons, the sharpening class division in the United States, and the failure of citizens to participate in democratic processes. This sense of urgency and crisis can help to create a readiness to design truly systemic reform.

We propose to now place the major responsibility for reform squarely in the laps of teachers. Why teachers? Intriguingly, although teachers represent the largest group of involved adults in the schools (other than parents) and the largest group of involved professionals, they are the only group that has not been charged with the responsibility for reform. The size of the workforce is not the only advantage that teachers bring to this undertaking. They represent the most stable group of professionals. Principals and other administrators come and go, yet teachers are usually in there for the long haul. With the exception of those who leave the profession early, teachers who decide to stay often remain in the same community. Furthermore, the teaching profession is the most politically powerful group in the education business. Nationally, the National Education Association and the American Federation of Teachers represent influential organizations that affect legislation and shape policy.

Yet even numbers, stability, and political influence are not enough to successfully undertake this daunting work. It will also take a new perspective, a different way of viewing the work of teaching and learning, schools and schooling, and the organization of power and authority in schools. We must reframe professional development as life's work and, in the process, build learning communities that are nurturing and growth producing, as well as challenging. This enterprise involves a new conception of the work of leading, conceived as a constructivist approach that engages colleagues as facilitators of each other's learning. This is what this book is about. In the following chapters, we will unfold a new reform agenda—the new road ahead—and invite teachers to take the reins.

Why This Book Was Written

This book grew out of conversations among its coauthors. As reformers, teachers, administrators, professors, and consultants, we found that we had a combined history of more than a century of experience with teaching and learning and with reform movements. As we reflected on these histories—some shared, some not—we found a compelling question that riveted our talk: Who *will* save our schools? We didn't hesitate. We each knew that it had to be the teachers. And we knew that doing business as usual and doing it better was not the answer. We trusted that some of the answers lay in our experiences and our current understandings. We began, together, to construct new understandings.

Linda Lambert, working with other colleagues (Deborah Walker, Diane Zimmerman, Joanne Cooper, Morgan Lambert, Mary Gardner, and P. J. Ford-Slack), had just finished *The Constructivist Leader* (1995). This work advances a new conception of leadership and leading that informs this present book. As chair of the Department of Educational Leadership at California State University, Hayward, she had worked with other colleagues to establish a constructivist program for preparing school administrators. Karen Kent brought years of experience in changing school cultures and leading significant systemic reform in schools. Michelle Collay and Anna Richert are on the frontlines every day in the preparation of teachers, watching them teach—and watching them struggle—watching them be enculturated in the old ways of doing business and struggling to teach them to teach differently. Mary Dietz is an international consultant with strong experience in constructivist learning for children and new forms of student and adult assessment. These convergent experiences and common understandings have created a compelling new look at the future of schooling and the role that teachers as leaders must assume in that future.

Who Should Read This Book and Why?

This book is written for teachers, teacher educators, staff developers, school and district administrators, parent educators, policymakers, and researchers—all those who have a stake in the future of our educational system. More specifically, it is written for those who are working with the lifelong professional development of teachers.

This book is unique in that it brings together a combination of ideas that have never been joined before: teaching as leading, constructivist leadership, an ecological perspective of systemic change, learning communities, and the professional development of teachers. This synthesis is different from the sum of its parts: Together, these ideas will form a new conception of teaching, learning, leading, and schooling and set a new stage for school reform.

About the Chapters

Chapter 1, "Examining the Context and Promise of Schooling," sets the scene for this book. We begin our journey on the new road ahead by describing the conditions, or context, of teaching and learning that have framed our assumptions and beliefs about what it is to teach in America. These context issues lead us to examine the nature of our changing society, the traditional patriarchy of schooling, our assumptions about teaching as a profession, and our failure to establish clear purposes for our work. We suggest that teachers will need to take primary responsibility for creating a new context for teaching and learning. And we advance the themes that will weave through the book and that will inform the perspectives and approaches that we are recommending. These themes include human learning and development, learning communities, constructivist leadership, and systemic change.

In Chapter 2, "The Teacher as Constructivist Leader," we define what we mean by "constructivist leadership" and "constructivist leading" by drawing parallels with constructivist learning. This approach that we have come to understand as making meaning of our learning, our work, is proposed as the central idea of leadership. If we view leading as facilitating the sense-making processes in our schools, we find that there are powerful implications for new roles, new work in shared leadership. We often think of leading as having direction—leading to where, for what purpose? This is also a key idea in our reconception of leadership, defined as the reciprocal learning processes among participants in a community. These processes enable those participants to construct meaning and knowledge together, leading toward the construction of a common purpose for schooling. Yet learning and purpose will not be accomplished unless we escape from an ancient view of schooling that has kept us locked into some old assumptions.

In Chapter 3, "Changing the System," we ask readers to step back and take a larger and different view of schooling. We propose an ecological perspective that will enable all members of school communities to engage in system reform. This perspective will construct a new set of relationships between educators and their communities. We will propose that we learn to organize ourselves into networks of relationships rather than hierarchies of established roles and authority. And we will describe what this perspective might look like as we rethink our school culture, curriculum and instruction, and accountability approaches in schools.

In Chapter 4, "Constructing Understandings of Learning Communities," we build on the premises in the preceding chapters in order to advance the learning community as the new context for teaching and learning. We describe learning communities and suggest why they have been so hard to attain. We will also challenge our readers to take on the charge of building such communities by suggesting how to go about the work. Finally, we will present several approaches from practice that have great promise for initiating and sustaining learning communities in schools.

Chapter 5, "Teaching as Leading," challenges us to not let go of our basic work—teaching—as we seek to lead. Our conception of leading as facilitating the learning processes among participants in a community honors teaching as leading. This chapter focuses on the teacher's leadership role as meaning maker with children and the teacher's role as meaning maker in school-level leadership. In fact, we believe that the parallel role between leadership with adults and leadership with children may emerge as the role of teacher leader.

We view these twin roles through the eyes of two sets of teachers: a group of novice teachers in their beginning years of teaching and a group of experienced teachers who begin to rethink their work as they venture out to complete a master's degree. We find in these personal experiences that the principles of constructivist education can offer a powerful catalyst for our thinking about the work of teachers and their roles as leaders.

In Chapter 6, "Who Sets the Learning Agenda," we examine those compelling ideas that drive the energy in our schools but are rarely spoken about. We look at both sides of power: power *over*, the urge to dominate, control, and direct; and power *with*, the engagement of members of community in their own learning, in creating their own destinies. We distinguish power from *authority*, that formal repository of power found in knowledge, roles, and positions; and we suggest that both are subject to being rethought and reframed. As we conclude Chapter 6, we are ready to draw forth the ideas in each chapter to describe the work of teacher leaders.

In Chapter 7, "Preparing the Constructivist Teacher Leader," we propose the commitments, knowledge, and skills that are essential for teachers as leaders. In order to consider learning as a continuous process of development, we situate ourselves at the intersection of school reform and professional development reform by again placing teacher learning at the center of the reform agenda. But this time, it is different. We will not propose teacher learning that will enable teachers to work well in the old system but teacher learning that will enable them to change the system. We will advance nine design principles for professional education. In drawing examples from practice, we will apply those principles to the work before us and suggest the reform of professional preparation programs.

Chapter 8, "The Future of Teaching, Leading, and Reform," is the capstone chapter in which we bring together our learnings from writing this book, anticipate some possible futures, and recommend significant alterations in policy and practice.

Linda Lambert
California State University
Hayward, California

Karen Kent
Bay Region IV Professional Development Consortium
San Mateo, California

Anna Ershler Richert
Mills College
Oakland, California

Michelle Collay
Hamline University
St. Paul, Minnesota

Mary E. Dietz
Frameworks
San Ramon, California

Acknowledgment

The authors want to thank their husbands and partners whose patience, understanding, and love made this work possible.

About the Authors

Linda Lambert, EdD, is Chair of the Department of Educational Leadership and Director of the Center for Educational Leadership at California State University, Hayward. These roles, and that of professor, have enabled her to work in numerous schools and districts, including Professional Development Schools. Before joining the faculty at CSUH, Linda was a teacher leader, principal, director, county professional development director, coordinator of academies, and designer of three major restructuring efforts. From 1989 to 1993, she worked in Egypt setting up a national curriculum center and in Thailand and Mexico in leadership development. The lead editor of the 1995 text, *The Constructivist Leader,* she has also written extensively about professional development and leadership. Her research and consultancy interests are in leadership, professional and organizational development, and school and district restructuring.

Karen Kent, EdD, is Director of the San Francisco Bay Region IV Professional Development Consortium. In her 16 years of experience in teacher-centered staff development, she has provided programs and participated in research focused on linking teacher involvement in whole school reform with professional development.

Anna Ershler Richert, PhD, is Associate Professor of Education at Mills College in Oakland, California, where she holds the Mary Metz Endowed Chair. She is Codirector of the "Teachers for Tomorrow's Schools" teacher credential and master's program. Her research on reflective practice and teacher learning at the preservice level has led to her new work on school reform and teacher learning in the context of school change. She sees learning as the key activity of teaching and welcomes this construction of leading that has learning at its core. She posts her hopes for school change on the processes of collaboration, learning, and leading and on the talented teachers who know how to do all three.

Michelle Collay, PhD, is Director of Graduate Education Programs at Hamline University in St. Paul, Minnesota. Faculty in Graduate Education work closely with practicing teachers undertaking graduate study who are committed to developing learning communities in their schools. Previously, she was a faculty member at the Center for Teaching and Learning at the University of North Dakota and Assistant Director of the Resident Teacher Program at the University of Oregon. Her research interests include teacher professional socialization, naturalistic inquiry and evaluation, school-university partnerships, and teacher leadership. Collay began her professional career as a music teacher in elementary and junior high school settings in California and Oregon.

Mary E. Dietz, MA, is a consultant who has focused her work on the continuous learning of professional educators and on how this learning fuels the change process in schools. She codesigned a program for the Facilitator Network, a group sponsored by the Delta Sierra Professional Development Consortium and the California Staff Development Council that supports substantive school change. As part of her efforts during the past eight years to foster adult learning, she published *Professional Development Portfolio: Facilitator's Guide* for designing and implementing portfolios.

Examining the Context and Promise of Schooling

TEACHING CAN BE A JOYFUL ENDEAVOR. A FULLY engaged child, eyes alight, can make teaching one of the most meaningful of all professions. Successes abound: a note from an appreciative parent, a lesson that went especially well, a child beginning to read for the first time, a colleague's asking eagerly for advice, sent a letter years later about an influence you had on a graduate's life. Such tributes are gems of acknowledgment that confirm your commitment to a profession of great worth.

Why do the rewards of such a profession not always seem enough? True, the material rewards are not great—but you knew that when you went into teaching. Something else feels awry; something is missing.

We will propose that part of the problem is that the context of teaching is often suffocating, frustrating, and even demeaning. And we will propose a new road ahead.

The "Context Clues" of Schooling

If you have ever worked with a child on reading skills—either formally or informally—you have undoubtedly made use of "context clues." Context clues can surround the reader with meanings that are already known so that the unknown can be made visible. The unknown, whether a word or a phrase, can gain meaning through inference. We can make sense of that word by figuring out what the writer figured out: What word would be needed here to complete the

meaning of the sentence or paragraph? Context clues also give meaning to our professional and personal lives.

In this chapter, we will set forth several "context clues" of teaching—those surrounding conditions that give meaning to this work
called teaching. We will suggest that these conditions have placed
teaching into a professional space in which the improvement of
schools has become nearly impossible. And we will propose conditions that we believe will change the context and realities of teaching
and therefore the quality of schooling. These promising conditions
will become the major themes in this book.

During this century, teaching has been defined and characterized
by historical and social context issues that have tightly bound the
work of teaching to common meanings for those in the profession
and those who would enter the profession. These attributes have
been imposed on teachers by society in its expectations of public
education, by organizational arrangements drawn from business
theory, and by those in the profession itself. Ironically, for context
issues to carry a heavy influence, they must be believed by those most
closely involved: the teachers themselves. Teachers have, by and
large, accepted their fate. They have struggled and resisted; but when
all is said and done, they have been willing (and able) to enculturate
the next generation of teachers into the profession as it exists today.
Why is this so?

We will suggest below a few significant context clues that can
shed some light on that question. These context issues have been
chosen for their inherent power in defining who we are as teachers,
the limits or boundaries imposed on our actions, and the futures that
we perceive.

Lack of a Clear Purpose for Schooling

Societies have long debated the purposes of schooling. Schooling
has been envisioned as producing the desired workforce, passing on
the learnings of the world's cultures (particularly Western Euro-
pean), controlling and bringing up our young, and teaching core values and moral behavior. Certainly all of these proposed purposes
play a vital role in our schools. We agree, however, with Jefferson as
quoted in Malone (1962, p. 448), Dewey (1938), Glickman (1993), and

multiple thinkers in between that our central purpose is the preparation of citizens who will actively develop and participate in a democratic society.

Rarely do the members of school communities engage in the necessary dialogue to examine, give meaning to, and act on a sense of clear purpose. Short of such dialogue—that requires time not consumed with information items—commitment to educational purpose continues to be weak and fragmented.

Educational Hierarchies

Since the days of the Egyptians and Romans, organizational ideas have tended toward amassing power and authority at the top of a hierarchy. The bureaucracy of schools creates conditions of social interaction that imitate factory hands in a production line (for a further discussion of the factory model, see Chapter 3). Those at the top have the right to direct the behaviors of those further down in the hierarchy. Because those at the bottom (factory workers, teachers, students) are always larger in number than those at the top, strategies have to be used to establish and maintain control. These strategies have involved rules, regulations, punishments, incentives, and cultures based on formal authority, patriarchy, and isolation. These ideas have become particularly fixed and unchallenged in public bureaucracies such as education. Issues of power and authority will be explored more thoroughly in Chapter 6.

Patriarchy as Leadership

The industrial model required a kind of leadership that involved authority over, not collaboration with. Those at the top of the hierarchy assumed patriarchal or matriarchal roles that created parent-child relationships among professional adults working in the same school community. Such relationships are characterized by permission asking and granting; punitive responses for slight transgressions (a look or word of disapproval, withholding of praise or resources, failure to ask favors); one-way evaluation, communication, and feedback; and praise or other extrinsic rewards. The results are predictable and are considered desirable by some members of the patriarchy or matriarchy: Teachers in these settings do not "grow up"; they do not progress through stages of adult development or become reflective practitioners. By design, the system promotes immaturity and stagnation. Yet teachers who report receiving recognition from administrators tend to stay in the profession (Shedd & Bacharach, 1991). One interpretation of this interesting finding is that those who prefer the patriarchal system stay in it, and those who remain in teaching expect administrators to provide extrinsic rewards. If they become administrators, they find it comfortable to dispense those rewards.

Many educators who were uncomfortable with the current system left the classroom to assume support roles and reform leadership roles or accepted leadership roles within local professional associations that sought to equalize power relationships (Gardner & Lambert, 1993).

Isolationism and Individualism

America's cultural heritage is particularly individualistic. Admiration for the "rugged individualist" saturated history books and early upbringing. A few professions—pioneering, farming, housewifery, teaching—offered the perfect home for the individualist who could "go it alone." Cut off from regular interaction with other adults, the individual teacher had to make it on his or her own. Throughout history, and even today, some find isolation slightly romantic; some feel they have no other choice but to isolate themselves; and others find isolation crippling to further growth and development as a teacher and as a professional.

Teaching as Women's Work

Historically, school leaders have been principals and superintendents who have exchanged interaction with children for hierarchical interaction with adults. This division of labor has also been related to gender (Bell & Chase, 1993; Bicklen, 1985; Grumet, 1980; Laird, 1988; Preston, 1991; Regan, 1990; Strober & Tyack, 1980). Throughout the century, teachers have been primarily women, whereas principals and superintendents have been primarily men. The lack of professional status for those who remain in teaching is reflected in current tensions that face teachers who choose to "stay in classrooms" yet fail to play the role that a mature professional could be expected to enact.

Only in recent decades have teachers remained in the profession for a lifetime. Before World War II, teachers were only marginally more educated than the students they taught, and most served the public for a short period of time. Females were seen as more pliant and more appropriate contributors to the moral development of society than males and were assumed to be marking time between their own schooling and family responsibilities (Carter, 1989; Cuban, 1984; Distad, 1994; Herbst, 1989; Lortie, 1975; Mattingly, 1975). The social expectation was that women would be supervised by those with more authority—the more highly educated and highly placed men. Whether it is the medical profession in Russia or teaching in America, professions that are largely populated by women hold lower status. The same conditions exist today in many parts of the United States and at the upper echelons of the hierarchy (superintendency level).

The Status of Schooling

Education is not among the more respected of professions: Indeed, many members of society do not view it as a profession at all. Teaching is viewed as women's work with children. The relatively low pay, lack of autonomy, centrally controlled curriculum, and blue-collar unionism have depressed the status of schooling to a lower level in our society than other professions.

One indicator of status is pay. Although teaching is among the lowest paid professions (superior only to the ministry), many point out that teachers actually work only about eight months of the year. Understandably, more salary is probably going to be tied to more time with children and more time in the kinds of collaboration with colleagues that bring improved teaching and learning.

A centrally or textbook-controlled or guided curriculum gives the impression of predictability, or certainty, of content (see following section), thus removing an essential opportunity to perform as a professional. Those of us in the teaching profession know that this predictability is more apparent than real. The more we learn about how learning occurs, the more we realize that any content must be mediated through existing experience, assumptions, and perceptions—which vary from child to child. The public does not have access to the same knowledge base that teachers do. This, of course, raises the issue of whose responsibility it is to educate the public, particularly parents, about the knowledge bases of teaching and the set of professional responsibilities that make up teachers' work.

Teaching as a Profession

The "blue-collar unionism" referred to above is a major roadblock in the development of teaching as a profession. Although national educational associations (NEA and AFT) pursue scholarly work, professional standards, inquiry, and publications, the factory model still persists at the local level. This approach cherishes the protection of teachers regardless of competence, salary, and working conditions (class size, transfer, and tenure policies). Although these are important issues, they must be held in balance with concerns for the quality of teaching, professional development, student learning (particularly for our diverse population), developing the next generation of teachers, and refining strategies such as shared decision making that promise to equalize power issues in schools. Teachers need to extend the agenda of their own unions and seek to establish increasingly professional associations.

The Myth of Certainty

An important tension exists between the uncertainty of school life and the regulated structures that characterize its form. By definition, schools are social institutions. The people and purposes they serve change as rapidly as the substance of their service and the methods for delivering it. Recent history provides many examples. For example, in California, changing demographics have altered the ethnic composition of most classrooms. Many children do not speak English as their first language—and even many of those who do arrive at school having had early life experiences very different from those of their teachers. Similarly, subject matters have changed and continue to change at startling rates. There has been an explosion of information in most disciplines. Rapid technological advancement has resulted in a national expectation of change in almost every arena of public life.

Located centrally in this cacophony of changing social forces, schools are, interestingly enough, quite resistant to change. Research on a century of progressive efforts in American education demonstrates little real (not symbolic) change. Furthermore, the change that has occurred has been (and continues to be) eschewed in favor of regulated systems of control designed to maintain the impression of certainty in the school context. Standards created in remote bureaucracies and rigid curricular mandates devoid of local input serve to control school personnel and processes and thus maintain an image of certainty in school organizations.

This myth of certainty can strangle a school's capacity for change. Risk taking is dangerous in a setting where prescribed outcomes are expected and where conformity, rather than curiosity, is valued. In most schools the curriculum is accepted as given, rather than uncertain; and even matters of pedagogy and management are mandated by direct mechanisms of regulation and control.

The Changing Demographics

As the myth of certainty prevails, the complexity of teaching is becoming significantly expanded by the changing demographics throughout the United States, where today, 30% of all school-age children come from language or racial minority groups (Futrell, 1994). Nearly 40% of children live in poverty, and 70% of children in urban centers are likely to attend school in run-down and inadequate facilities. Many of these schools focus on rote memorization, drill, and discipline. Poor children and minority children are far more likely to be taught by unqualified teachers (Kozol, 1991). These children are actually deprived of community, because instruction still emphasizes traditional, unproductive approaches such as the acquisition of basic skills and factual knowledge through individual structured activities and repetitive drill (Oakes, 1985).

Diversity in culture, language, learning styles, parent support, and resources creates daily experiences for teachers that are overwhelming. Strategies and priorities that stood us in good stead over the years simply do not work in today's schools.

The Punitive Society

The tendency to punish transgression from the norm—a legacy of our Puritan history—has informed our structures and our relationships. Teachers have tended to assume the same role with children that those higher on the hierarchical ladder have assumed with them: control and patriarchy. Within a setting of one teacher to 30 children, teachers have also looked to strategies involving "rules, regulations, punishments, incentives, and cultures based on formal authority, patriarchy, and isolation" (see previous section, "Educational Hierarchies"). School staffs often look to discipline codes and rules as the first step to school improvement.

Our unique histories have ushered in a 1990s society in which we are spending more for prisons than for schools. During the past decade in California, 19 prisons have been built, but only one state university. There were more persons in prison for drug offenses in 1995 than the entire prison population of 1981 (Schiraldi, 1995). Although we have significant knowledge about how to prevent addiction and failure and how to build resiliency and achievement through "front loading" early support for children and families, we fail to provide the resources to do so. Why is this? Our former students— now our citizens—were raised in institutions where transgression from the norm (might it be creativity or preference?) was met with punishment rather than with options, where sustainable relationships were broken by grade-level progression, and where meaningful contributions and responsible actions were taken only by adults.

In striking contrast, we now recognize that a strong, caring community plays an important role in the lives of children who are perceived as the most at risk. Community, as opposed to punishment, can actually mitigate the negative effects of poverty on students (Battistich, Solomon, Kim, Watson, & Schaps, 1995).

The Emergence of Teacher Leadership

Education reforms in the past decade have necessitated teacher leadership or at least involvement. School-based management, shared decision making, school improvement, school site councils and advisory boards, and program reviews all call for the involvement of teachers. In a few cases, these involvements have been authentic, resulting in a genuine shift of power and authority. In more cases, however, these reforms have been only pro forma, applying the letter rather than the intent of the reform. In these instances, teachers still have access to limited information (particularly about resources) and contribute in a consultative fashion to technical, rather than substantive, decisions. Without opportunities to build the capacity for working collaboratively, systemic change is not possible.

In locales where teacher leadership is actually emerging, backlash factors are heavy. Teachers undermine other teachers who violate the myth of equity; administrators feel threatened by loss of authority and power; some teachers and administrators long for the comfort of autocratic leadership. Teacher leadership, as we will discuss it in this book, requires a redefinition of everyone's role: teacher, administrator, student, and parent.

The Context of Schooling: What Does It Mean?

All teaching occurs in a context or a series of nested contexts that affect how, and toward what end, the work of teaching is accomplished. We have examined the relationship between context and teaching by setting forth several conditions that influence the profession of teaching. We propose that a composite portrait is emerging. Teaching can be viewed as

> *a quasi-profession of relatively low status in today's society that is primarily composed of women who find themselves embedded in patriarchal and unionized systems at the bottom of an educational hierarchy. Confronted with a complex, often impossible job, teachers perceive themselves as having few options, little support from colleagues, and lacking a sense of collective purpose that could contribute to substantial improvement in their work lives and in the learning of children.*

In this portrait lies the fate of our children; in this portrait lies both the reason for the failure of reform and the possibility for the success of schooling in America. In this book, we invite you to consider that the hope for our schools is set squarely in the hands of the teaching profession. As we noted in the Preface, teachers are the most numerous, stable, experienced, and politically powerful group of educators—so why not engage teachers as reform leaders? Full engagement of teachers in the reform effort can enhance the leadership capacity of schools so that they can struggle with tough issues, find common purpose, and get the work done.

To assert this responsibility, we will ask teachers to work together with each other, as well as with administrators, parents, students, and community members to alter the context of schooling. This is a large task; it stretches beyond the bounds of the classroom and requires some new understandings and commitments. However, we are persuaded that unless these contextual issues can be jointly addressed, we will not succeed with children. The "new road ahead" involves some new themes or perspectives as well as some with which teachers are well acquainted. Familiar and new themes need to be combined into new frameworks for thinking about schooling—a few new bottles—a new context for action.

The Road Ahead: New Themes

Several themes or perspectives will be described, deepened, and sustained throughout this book. These themes will advance new promises for finally achieving the reforms that will save our schools. They will enable us to address the leadership capacity of school and society and the role of the teaching profession in that endeavor. The themes are assumptions that embrace learning, leading, community, and change.

Human Learning and Development

Children and adults learn primarily through a process known as "constructivism." Constructivism assumes that all learners come to the learning situation with prior experiences, assumptions, beliefs, and perceptions. Within a cultural and historical context, learners engage together with new information and knowledge, puzzling circumstances, and dilemmas and questions and seek to "make sense of" the new ideas. This "making sense of" or "construction" requires

that learners alter their current mental models to connect prior learnings with new learnings.

Accumulated learnings are continually reinterpreted in the light
of new ideas, growing maturity, and the capacity of the community
to learn together. For instance, new information about students can
cause teachers to rethink strategies that may have proven successful
at an earlier time. A critical role played by colleagues and peers is to
challenge and refine current assumptions through dialogue, reflection, and shared inquiry.

Recent brain research has given renewed credibility to our understandings of constructivism. We now know that the brain is a plastic
rather than a fixed organ, which continues to develop throughout our
lifetime. Small infants require stimulation and engagement, as do
older adults. As the brain grows, it forms relational maps that connect
ideas and understandings together (construction), and it develops
increasingly complex networks of relationships among these ideas.
These ideas are imbued with meaning as they make sense to the
learner. The images of the learner's brain as "empty vessel," "blank
slate," or even "computer" are archaic and without supporting evidence.

Furthermore, as humans learn together in communities, they experience what are sometimes thought of as "higher stages of human
development." We have come to understand that both individual
and group learning are essential to the processes of development and
can happen fully only in community. Interestingly, these stages
tend to enable learners to converge around common values that
include equity, caring, and social justice (Gilligan, 1982; Kegan, 1982;
Kohlberg, 1976; Loevinger, 1976). These common values focus and
deepen the sense of collective purpose in schools.

The Learning Community

A learning community is an ecosystem; that is, its participants
are interdependent and connected in their learning and work. When
some participants learn, others also learn and benefit; when problems stay unresolved, the whole community suffers. The whole of
the community is greater than the sum of its parts: What we accomplish as a group exceeds the sum of our individual efforts. Interdependent communities tend to organize themselves around key

ideas and issues. These ideas will be explained in depth as *systems thinking* in Chapter 3, where we will describe how these ideas can form in communities called "school."

We realize that there are multiple forms and definitions of community. Communities can be cults that are limiting or even abusive of human learning and development. We speak here of many forms of *moral communities*—communities in which the central purpose is focused on core values that cherish and care about the learning and development of its members. In such communities, members derive moral direction from each other and contribute moral energy to the whole. Moral communities are referred to in this book in several ways:

- *Learning community* refers to the processes and relationships among members that enable the entire community to learn and grow. These processes and relationships involve inquiry, dialogue, reflection, and action.
- *Professional community* primarily concerns educators involved in the shared work of developing the profession of teaching.
- *School community* refers to open boundaries of community membership and includes educators, children and their families, and members of the broader community as well.

Constructivist Leadership

Teachers as leaders need to facilitate reciprocal learning processes among participants in a school community. To lead is to attend to the learning of those around us as well as to the culture of the whole organization. Reciprocity is a central concept in the process of learning together in community because it requires the give and take of those with more or less equal power and authority. Anything short of reciprocity gives rise to the problems of paternalism in which one person has more expertise, authority, status than another and sees his or her role as "helping" those less able. Reciprocity assumes that we have something to learn from each other as well as something to give to each other.

Teachers, as natural learners, are also natural leaders. In Chapter 2, we will describe "constructivist leadership" in detail, including the understandings and skills of emerging teacher leaders. Furthermore, we will argue that when many community members are involved in the processes of leadership, the capacity of the school to lead itself grows exponentially.

Systemic Change

Change is the natural state of our world. But change is perceived differently in interdependent learning communities than in schools that separate people by role, age, function, room, schedule, and tradition. In schools in which staffs have the feeling of fragmentation and overload, change just seems like another thing on their plates—another project to carry out, another disconnected task to check off the list. In schools in which change is the natural outgrowth of learning, there is a flow, an unfolding of next steps that makes sense because these steps have emerged from dialogue, reflection, and shared inquiry. Communities that have built learning into their ways of doing business together are resilient, capable of responding to crises and struggles without being dismantled by them.

This constructivist process of change is learning. As we learn together, we change—and so does our community and our work. Such change does not come from a workshop, a newly imposed objective, or an isolated decision. Natural change is *systemic:* It is connected to everything else. Natural change does not evoke crippling resistance but results from a feeling that "this makes sense." Change that grows out of our work together may take the form of long-term or short-term adaptations, leading to evolutionary change in the entire system.

In each chapter, our assumptions about change will become more clear as we provide scenarios and invite you to draw from experiences in which change was the outgrowth of learning.

Toward a Vision of Teaching as Leading

We are asking teachers to work with others to alter the context in which they work in order to alter learning for students and adults. This new context is a learning community, led by teachers, administrators, parents, and students, in which dialogue, reflection, and shared inquiry are the norm. We envision teaching as a profession of educational leaders committed to the learning of the students they serve and of each other.

This book brings together several sets of ideas about schools, change, and leadership. We envision schools, seen as constantly developing systems of interdependent entities, as being led primarily by teachers with the active participation of their colleagues (administrators, parents, students, and community members). Our idea of leadership rests on a belief that couples leading and learning. As teachers work together to guide the inevitably changing system of which they are a part, they create a community of learners who engage in constructing knowledge and defining collective purpose. These working relationships among teachers are both reciprocal and coevolutionary (growing together); within their context, learning occurs. In our emerging conception, then, teachers who create and nurture these relationships and the opportunities embedded in them for learning are leaders. As leaders and learners, they work together in interdependent ways to direct the work of this dynamic, changing system called school.

Such action requires all participants in the processes of learning, leading, and changing to understand the school community as a whole, to see their work as systemically connected. This focus can mobilize the energies of school staffs around the work that they value most, bringing a clarity of purpose and a sense of efficacy to the profession of teaching.

The Teacher as Constructivist Leader

ALL OF US KNOW WHAT IT IS TO LEAD AT ONE time or another. It might have been in Scouts, 4-H, or soccer. It might have been by arranging a class party when we were in the fourth grade, by leading a basketball team in high school, or by working with other mothers or fathers in a cooperative nursery school. Over the years we have developed our ideas about leadership. At some point, we may have decided, "I am a leader" or "I am not a leader." This decision, much like other significant decisions in our lives—"I am not creative," "I am a good problem solver," "I don't do well under stress"—has determined our fate and influenced us as teachers.

If you decided early on that you were a leader, we would like you to read this chapter with this question in your mind: How can I become a better leader? If you decided that you were not a leader, please open your mind to the possibility of changing this perception.

In our first chapter, we described the context in which we write about teacher leadership—its dilemmas, issues, problems. Throughout this text, we will confront these dilemmas, offering fresh perspectives, alternative interpretations, and new possibilities. This chapter will propose a new conception of teacher leadership, one that links learning and leading as firmly together as teaching and leading. We believe that the work of teaching is learning and that the work of leading is learning as well. The work of leading is everyone's work.

As we begin this discussion, it may be useful to recall together the historical context in which we find ourselves.

The Evolution of Our Thinking
About Learning and Leading

For centuries, humankind has struggled with the notion of learning. Historically, learning meant that a certain body of knowledge, sometimes called "the canon" and most often drawn from Western thought, was obtained through memorization and drill. In some mysterious way, these memorized ideas were to become ours and subsequently make us wise, skilled, and competent.

Authority rested in this canon, in the institutions that protected and promoted it (the schools and the church), and of course, in the role of the teacher. With this thing called the canon under his or her arm, the teacher entered a classroom where receptive and compliant students eagerly waited. The work of the teacher was to deliver, insert, tell these students the information, which they were to memorize and recite, eventually parroting back in as exact a form as possible. This was fairly straightforward. Teacher and student roles were well understood, as was the role of knowledge.

During this century, advances in psychology and testing ushered in the concept of *behaviorism*. Behaviorism told us that human behavior was predictable and controllable. The more we learned about human behavior and what made people "tick," the more precisely we could control the behavior of students and set boundaries for classroom conduct and deportment. Behavior could be controlled best if the teacher knew the "ability" of the students and therefore could diagnose and treat (or intervene) in ways that would ensure that the teachings were appropriately learned. This mechanistic view of the world and of people as predictable, controllable machines will be further challenged by our work in systemic thinking in the next chapter.

The development of specific tests of intelligence (IQ) by psychologists such as Binet and Thorndike enabled the profession and the society to test; diagnose abilities; and classify, sort, and treat specific persons in different ways. Abilities were thought to be innate and fixed. Students were thought to have a limited range of possibilities, because potential was limited by ability.

During the succeeding decades, the profession proved clever in applying these ideas to schools. Children were sorted and grouped by ability. "Tracks" enabled schools to organize and deliver "appropriate" instruction. Schools were organized like factories: Students marched from grade to grade like assembly lines in which each year a "new piece" was added. Many students, particularly girls and minorities, were given consistent advice about their career and life choices that reflected the society's understandings of both roles and abilities. Historically (as well as today) many schools succeeded—for about 30% of the population. Others dropped out, either literally or figuratively.

Behaviorism was raised to a new and more useful level of development during the 1970s by the "effectiveness movement." Seeking schools that succeeded with minority children, Ron Edmonds (1979) identified elementary schools in which minority children performed adequately on standardized tests in reading and math. The behaviors and practices in these schools were identified as "effectiveness factors": strong leadership on the part of the principal, direct instruction, parent involvement, safe and orderly climate. Despite the progress made in looking at the whole school (rather than just separate programs), the hierarchical model of schooling was still assumed: a strong principal directing the work of others. These effectiveness factors became the basis for the training of administrators and the development of many staff development programs. If administrators and teachers could perform these behaviors successfully, their schools would also succeed. Sometimes this training helped; sometimes it didn't. Learning the behaviors of others in order to insert them into your own environment fails to take into consideration the role of context and the learning of the adults and children working together in that unique setting.

During the past 15 years, we have seen a shift in our thinking about learning with such ideas as a "community of learners" and a "learning community" (see Chapter 4). These ideas include a basic assumption that learning is primarily a social endeavor and is context-dependent—that is, it grows differently in different settings and with different people. And when people work toward a common purpose together, they become committed to the learning they achieve. Cooperative learning, integrated curriculum, community projects, and smaller units of students and teachers all emerged from these understandings.

The "learning community" philosophy is informed by a different notion of learning than the behaviorism that we spoke of earlier. This notion is known as "constructivism" and represents a strong, parallel movement to the behaviorist practices used throughout this century.

Mary Catherine Bateson (1994) points out that "human beings construct meaning as spiders make webs—or as appropriate enzymes make proteins" (p. 52). Meaning making is an active process; it is motion, and it is natural. The meaning-making mechanism, like web building, is built into our brains. This understanding of learning as meaning making and as relational (recall the functioning of the brain) is the basis of what we have come to call *constructivist learning.*

As we described in Chapter 1, constructivist theory recognizes that the learner comes to any experience with his or her own history, experience, perceptions, and beliefs. This commonsense observation has changed our prior ideas about learning because no person views the world in quite the same way. Our uniqueness determines how we interpret the world around us. If we view learning as the unfolding and development of our unique perceptions and interpretations of the world, then it follows that to teach is to mediate, to connect, new experiences with prior perceptions so that we will never think in quite the same way again. Our worldviews have been altered or reinforced. For instance, a child who believes that the sun goes down and the moon comes up may not be persuaded by different information unless she talks it through with a teacher and classmates in ways that allow her to make sense of the new information and how it challenges her previous assumptions. In the same way, a teacher may not be able to examine her ideas about the capacity of boys and girls to learn English until she and her colleagues discover new information together and talk it through.

Dewey (1916, 1938) was the first to make the dramatic case that learning had to be active, drawing generously from the learner's own experiences. But it was Piaget who described what he considered to be the biological nature of learning: An organism (learner) encounters new experiences and events and seeks to assimilate these into existing cognitive structures or to adjust the structures to accommodate the new information. Piaget saw children as moving through stages of development as active scientists interacting with and constructing theories about their environments, reflecting on and struggling with disequilibrium, and creating new ways of thinking. It was Piaget who first used the word *constructivism*, and it was the early childhood movement that imported his work into education in the United States (DeVries & Kohlberg, 1987).

Jerome Bruner added important dimensions to Piaget's work by emphasizing the role of social interaction, history, and language in the learning process (Bruner, 1966; Bruner & Haste, 1987). Furthermore, Bruner introduced Lev Vygotsky, a Russian psychologist, to educators in the United States. Vygotsky had independently arrived at the conclusion that people construct meaning and knowledge together and do so within the context of their historical and cultural histories (Vygotsky, 1962, 1978). Children or adults may interact with others in a cooperative learning situation, continually receiving informal feedback to their thinking, being stimulated by other perspectives, and hearing conflicting interpretation of ideas. As these learners make sense of what they are experiencing, their sense making is filtered through cultural norms and historical experiences that influence the conclusions they draw. Each interaction, like a spiraling pool of ideas, challenges and forms their thinking further. Vygotsky (1978) realized that all learning appears first at the social level and then at the individual level.

We now know that learning is learning, whether it occurs in children or adults. Although adults bring more history, more experiences, and more reasoned beliefs to the learning experience, the processes of learning still entail the collective and individual construction of meaning and knowledge. Like learners of all ages, adults learning together create shared histories, cultures, and purposes.

We like to think of leading as attending to the learning of colleagues. In this way, leading facilitates the learning that results in the development of purposeful learning communities.

What Is Constructivist Leadership?

If leading is viewed as facilitating the learning of colleagues in a community, it becomes not only a feasible endeavor for teachers but a moral imperative. It is essential that everyone in a school community engage in leadership that enables its participants to construct meaning and knowledge together. From such collective meaning making (Senge, 1990) comes the possibility of a purposeful community—one that succeeds with all of its children and adults.

We have great faith in the capacity of humans to develop purposeful communities. The creation of a shared purpose grows out of the conversations of responsible adults who are invested in the growth and development of each other, the students, and the school community.

Recall the time when you decided to go into teaching. Certainly it was not because of the promised income or status. What differences did you expect to make? What sense of purpose drove your decision? We all come to our work in education with a personal sense of purpose or vision. The core values that drive our need to make a difference are always with us. Sometimes they seem buried by the dailiness of work in schools. When they do, we often find conditions that Duke (1994) refers to as "drift" and "detachment." Drift is that rudderless feeling we get when we feel directionless, without purpose. Detachment is how we often cope with this purposelessness. We detach ourselves emotionally from our work, going through the motions but lacking a commitment to learning and community.

When purpose is not made explicit, we feel fragmented. Our plates may be full of disconnected, separate tasks—a new reading and math program, parent participation, health lessons, a program review portfolio, discipline problems, science units, self-esteem lessons, conflict resolution. All are valid undertakings, but unless they are integrated into a whole, they can be overwhelming and lead to disillusionment, fatigue, and burnout.

On the other hand, when participants in a school community work together to resurface, share, and act on their senses of purpose, the work of teaching and learning takes on more meaning: It makes sense. This process of making sense of our work together is constructivist learning.

When we learn in a constructivist mode, we begin with purpose, beliefs, assumptions, and experiences. We ground ourselves in who we are, honoring where we've been, so that together we can discover new ways of being. We find that teachers are qualified to facilitate this kind of learning for and with each other. Hence, a constructivist leader facilitates learning processes that enable participants in a community to construct meanings—to learn together—leading to a shared purpose of schooling.

We find it useful to distinguish between leadership and leaders. We think of *leadership* as the reciprocal processes that enable participants in a community to construct meanings that lead toward a shared purpose of schooling (Lambert et al., 1995). Leadership is not a person or a role. It is the processes that make up the relationships among us. In other words, leadership is the participatory learning opportunities that exist among us in a school culture. A *leader*, on the other hand, is someone—anyone in the school community—who facilitates the processes among us. This someone can be a teacher or an administrator, a parent, a community member, or a student.

The distinction between leadership and leader is important if we are to create a new understanding of leading. For decades we have used these terms interchangeably, and this has led us in directions that are limiting rather than expanding. The most harmful of these paths has been the insistence on the "great man or woman" theory that argues that an extraordinary, charismatic leader rises to the top to assume leadership. This idea has caused many with important gifts to withdraw from leading, thus abdicating both their opportunities and their responsibilities. For instance, if you acknowledged at the beginning of this chapter that you did not see yourself as a leader, it may have been a decision made in the shadow of a charismatic leader.

If we think of constructivist leaders as "participants in a school community," this can mean all of us. We use the word *participants* to communicate the idea of equity and shared responsibilities. The traditional and archaic terms *leaders and followers* "conjure up images of walking behind, being alert to the cue of the 'real' leader, waiting one's turn" (Lambert et al., 1995). These are not images that are useful to shared leadership. "Participantship" implies that each person has opportunities to perform leadership behaviors that benefit the community as a whole. This perception can significantly alter our notions of roles in schools. As we will see, these behaviors are accessible to all teachers as they develop in their professional work.

We include in our definition of leadership some of the reciprocal processes and patterns that can cause learning and establish communities. These processes that enable are referred to here as the "reciprocal processes" of leadership. Although these processes are varied and many, we refer here to reciprocal processes directly tied to constructivist learning. Additional approaches and strategies are suggested in Chapter 4.

Reciprocity means that we listen to each other, give and receive somewhat equally, and learn from each other. Such relationships require a capacity to care for self and others, to understand that our own growth and that of others is interconnected. For instance, teachers who participate in peer coaching bring both an expertise and an openness to this trusting relationship. An awareness of what we do know can provide expertise to another; an increasing awareness of what we don't know can cause us to be open to new learnings. In reciprocal relationships, we are sometimes givers and sometimes receivers. Relationships that are dominated by one role or another are deeply unsatisfying. Over time, they result in paternalistic relationships that establish dependencies and resentment. Authentic relationships, as we shall see below, involve the realignment of power (see Chapter 6) so that participants can emerge into leadership roles whereby they share more or less equally in guiding one another to new meanings.

For instance, in our work with professional development schools, we are learning that senior teachers are taking responsibility for the development of the next generation of teachers—sometimes even by voluntarily teaching the toughest classes so that they will not be assigned to new teachers. New teachers are bringing to these relationships a freshness of perspective along with a reverence for the experiences of their senior mentors.

In *The Constructivist Leader,* Lambert and her colleagues (1995) refer to reciprocal processes of leadership that

- evoke potential in a trusting environment;
- reconstruct, "break set" with, old assumptions and myths;
- focus on the construction of meaning; and
- frame actions that embody new behaviors and purposeful intentions.

The phrase "evoke potential in a trusting environment" can be understood when we consider human potential as being composed of the myriad of memories, experiences, perceptions, prior knowledge, assumptions, and beliefs that make up who we are—our schema or worldview. Our beliefs are the chief screen or lens through which we interpret reality. We have often observed teacher groups make progress toward shared curriculum work only to disband when they get to the specifics of the work. This occurs when teachers do not bring to the surface and discuss their underlying beliefs about curriculum and instruction. Disagreements are almost always about underlying assumptions and beliefs. When we work together to call forth what we believe, we can honestly confront why we think the way we do.

How often have we attended a staff development workshop in which the trainer tells us about a new idea? Little do others know about what we already think and believe. New approaches in the use of constructivism in professional development are highly promising (Sparks, 1995), and these approaches are essential to our daily lives in school as well. It is essential that the learning processes of working together in schools be understood as "professional development" (Lambert, 1988, 1989). Our regular conversations about school problems and dilemmas need to include the surfacing of our experiences and beliefs if we are to understand how we currently approach our work and how we interpret our observations. For instance, if our experiences have not included working with Latino children, it may not occur to us to ask certain questions, to look for unexpected responses in teaching situations, or to question how we define learning for all children.

To "reconstruct, 'break set' with, old assumptions and myths" begins to happen when we bring them to our awareness, usually in the form of questions. These questions can guide our inquiries, perhaps in the form of examining student work, doing action research, disaggregating school data, talking with students and parents, visiting other schools, reading research articles, joining networks. Our questions—How do we know children are learning? How do we accomplish literacy for all third graders? What strategies work well with language minority children?—can also provide the appropriate opening for staff training in ideas that now have become the center of our inquiry, rather than "training" that someone else decides is important.

As we discover new or different information, we are called on to reexamine our interpretations of previous experiences and thus our beliefs, perceptions, and assumptions. This is tough work and must be done within a community that shares awarenesses about what learning means, how it is affecting them, and how they garner appropriate support for the complex work of teaching. Without a supportive learning community, we tend to deny, avoid, or rationalize information that causes us discomfort.

As a continuing link in the learning process, to "focus on the construction of meaning" means to jointly make sense of what we are learning. How does this information about Latina girls change how we interpret what we see? Have we altered our expectations for parents based on what we now know? Does this fit together? What new assumptions do I now hold about my students? Are there new approaches that occur to us for working with African American boys that we hadn't thought of before?

A teacher at Chavez Elementary School told the following story. This scenario combines the first three reciprocal processes and leads us to understand the fourth as well:

> At Chavez Elementary School, we historically lowered grades when homework was not handed in. We assumed several things about the process of assigning and doing homework. To us, completed homework meant that the concepts were being learned through additional practice, that the student was being responsible, and that the regularity of homework was building self-discipline that would benefit children in future years as well (and, of course, an assumption that is very difficult to face: that grades are good measures of abilities and performances).
>
> One afternoon in a faculty meeting, we were expressing our usual frustrations over the homework dilemma when Maria Sanchez said, "Why don't we challenge ourselves to think differently about this problem?" The silence in the room was suffocating. John Curry finally said, "What do you mean, Maria?" Maria explained that we all seemed to hold the same ideas about homework and its values. "What if we set those ideas aside," she said, "and really found out what is going on?"
>
> After further discussion, the faculty formed a study group that designed a study in which each person could participate. The study involved interviewing students and parents, documenting homework patterns (who did what and when), comparing differences among cultural groups in their responses to homework, reading the research literature on homework, and talking with staff from other schools that

had encountered and worked through this problem. Their findings were dramatic: (a) In homes in which parents worked with their children on homework, the children handed it in and did better overall in school. (b) In ethnic and cultural minority homes, the findings were even more powerful. Where parents worked with the children at home, children did significantly better than their peers.

At the next staff development day, the staff examined the findings and the patterns of behavior they observed. They also explored their own assumptions and the typical responses that had been the norm of the years. They found little relationship between their responses and either the causes or results of homework performance. Their conversations brought them face to face with their own expectations and relationships with parents. By the end of the day, they outlined a tentative plan for building a partnership with parents as coteachers. The actual plan, they knew, must substantially involve parents in the planning.

The findings of this study at Chavez enabled the staff to "frame actions that embodied new behaviors and purposeful intentions." Not only did they shift their focus from individual student as the villain in the homework drama to the parent-child relationship in the home, but they also realized that parents had to be full partners in their planning processes as well. They needed to let go of some long-held assumptions about responsibility, punishment, and assessment.

The capacity of a staff to undertake and succeed with such an undertaking is made possible by leadership from all members of the school community and continuing support of each other during the process. Framing and implementing new actions are essential if constructivist learning is to make a difference in the school. These differences give rise to a cumulative understanding of the community's shared purpose as the staff is challenged to alter actual practices. Teachers and administrators facilitate these processes by asking questions, giving feedback, engaging in dialogue, negotiating conflict, and suggesting courses of action. When they do so, we would consider them constructivist leaders.

How Do Constructivist Leaders
Reframe Roles and Relationships?

We have alluded often to the issue of roles. Roles tend to confine and define who we are, whether it be as wives or husbands, daughters or sons, mothers or fathers, administrators, teachers, or students. The confinement comes from how we define ourselves and, equally so, how others define us. Roles are predictable, often holding us prisoners to old ways of thinking. How many of us have returned to our hometowns—for some of us a small Midwestern town—only to be treated as we were as youths? Roles can be particularly difficult to rethink if we choose to work and live in the same place throughout our careers.

Roles determine how we interact with each other, what we talk about, what we don't talk about, and how we behave. Attempts to break out of our established roles can be threatening to others and frightening to ourselves. This is part of what makes shared leadership so difficult. Yet to create relationships that are different, roles must be redefined. Becoming full participants requires that we learn our way into new definitions of ourselves and our work.

Traditionally, relationships, particularly in institutions such as schools, have been governed by rules and fragmentation. Teacher evaluation, contracts, personnel procedures, budget management, and time schedules are dominated by rules that define relationships in schools. Even though these blockades may offer a transitory illusion of security, they can also contribute to drift and detachment. These blockades are often organized into rigid role descriptions (administrator, teacher, aide) that get in the way of our working and learning. The challenge of reframing roles and relationships is embedded in the challenge of reframing leadership itself.

Constructivist leaders facilitate our shared learning experiences in schools. We've described our first undertaking in "reciprocal processes" of learning as evoking potential in ourselves and others. What do we evoke? What are those inner resources that are called forth as we learn? What behaviors and characteristics emerge in our relationships with each other that are beyond our expectations, even may surprise us?

The concept of *emergence* in biology may help us to think about this process. *Emergent evolution* is a theory holding that "completely new kinds of characteristics appear at certain stages of the evolutionary process, usually as a result of an unpredictable arrangement of preexisting elements" (*American Heritage Dictionary*; Soukhanov & Severynse, 1992).

New characteristics and behaviors come into existence as we learn together. This emergence of new behaviors or characteristics arises when the elements in our relationships—in our interactions with each other ("the unpredictable arrangement of preexisting elements")—enable us to learn together. As we enter into dialogue together, inquire into practice, and collectively reflect on and make sense of our work, we evoke our own human potential—we emerge into new definitions of our roles as teachers, as leaders.

In professional development schools in Richmond and Hayward, California, we noticed that teachers began to "self-organize" as their roles changed. We use the idea of self-organization (see Chapter 3) to mean that teachers suggested other ways of organizing themselves to get their work done: Ninth-grade core teachers met for a day of dialogue and planning; kindergarten through third-grade teachers formed study groups around key planning components; a math department did a self-analysis of their needs and sought external members on their teams.

The staff at Chavez Elementary emerged into new definitions of what it is to be a teacher, a professional educator. Their shared learning processes evoked inner resources from all of them that reframed their roles and therefore the meanings they brought to the work of teaching. A few of these inner resources included the courage to challenge norms and practices, an interest in inquiring into practice, and a willingness to hold up their own beliefs to scrutiny. These teachers began to see themselves as part of a larger whole, as part of a community that could meet and solve tough problems together—essential conditions for leadership roles.

In reframing roles, relationships are reframed as well. This is a dynamic process: New roles necessitate new relationships, and new relationships can create the consciousness necessary to carve out new roles.

Mary Poplin and her colleagues (1993), in an important study known as "Voices from the Inside," point out that there is a deep absence of authentic relationships in schools. Often school community members do not feel "trusted, given responsibility, spoken to honestly and warmly, and treated with dignity and respect." Maxine Greene (1988) refers to the community that we create together as involving possibilities for an authentic presence with each other, as "being real and vulnerable with each other in ways that engage us in genuine conversations" (Lambert, 1995, p. 33). Being real and vulnerable with each other allows public meaning making to take place. Kegan (1982) describes meaning making as one of the most intimate of human actions.

What is an "authentic relationship"? Certainly the language of trust, responsibility, honesty, warmth, dignity, and respect captures some vital aspects of authenticity. We would suggest that there are additional dimensions that are critical as well if such relationships are to form the essential patterns of a learning community in which we evolve, emerge, and grow together:

- Holding a long-term investment and concern for the growth and development of colleagues, students, and parents: It is important to invest in each other for the long haul, not just during certain events or experiences such as a program quality review
- Learning from each other in reciprocal relationships, for reciprocity distributes power and authority more equally
- Providing sustained support for other members of the community by being there for each other
- Insisting on the growth of each other by holding and exercising high expectations: This involves both congeniality (getting along together) and collegiality (challenging each other to be our best)
- Seeking truths together, trying to figure out how things are really working in the school: Are children learning? How do we know?
- Creating collective memories together and respecting, but not becoming stuck in, these shared experiences
- Understanding the need for multiple patterns of relationships that nourish a purposeful community; working with different

groups of teachers around different tasks or issues; making an effort to work with those who think and believe somewhat differently from us

- Seeking meaning together so that relationships and communities make sense: This idea is at the heart of constructivist learning

These dimensions of authentic relationships require a significant change in roles. The reframing of professional roles can occur as people literally grow into new ideas about what it is to be a teacher or an administrator.

Extensive research into teacher leadership (Blackford, 1995) has helped us to understand that at least three role shifts need to take place for teacher leadership to be successful in schools:

1. A formal establishment of teacher leader roles
2. The development of leadership behaviors among all teachers
3. A redefinition of the role of the principal to one that is collaborative and inclusive

Once again, we find that this "three-legged stool" forms a dynamic: If any piece is missing, the emergence of leadership is slowed or even reversed.

In the first instance, *roles are created* that are larger than the current perception of the role of teacher currently held by the teacher. Those who choose these roles literally grow into the role, filling the spaces between the current conception of self and the new expectations. As a junior high school principal, Lambert worked with faculty to create new roles for the emerging leaders that we recognized on the staff. Although they had no financial or other resources for these teachers, they found that titles, job descriptions, and authority created the roles quite successfully (e.g., Student Leadership Coach, Peer Coaching Coordinator, Core Team Leader).

In the case of the *broad-based development of leadership behaviors,* teachers emerge into new and continually expanding roles by the very nature of learning to see themselves differently and therefore behaving differently. (They also do not sabotage those in other leadership roles.) Throughout this book, we will suggest leadership commitments, knowledge, and skills needed by all teachers.

The third shift, the *role of the principal,* is one of the most important to be redefined—and in some ways the most difficult. The difficulty flows not just from the complexity of the proposed new roles but also from the predictable reticence about the changes that many incumbents will feel. Some will construe the new coleader role as a downgrading from the simpler, more comfortable hierarchical status currently enjoyed. To the contrary, the role of a collaborative leader seeking to facilitate truly systemic change is infinitely more challenging, more complex, and ultimately more significant than the traditional role. For those who bet on the principal as the most important school change agent, the stakes simply get higher.

Nationwide, many preparatory programs are guiding the development of school administrators who are collaborative, inclusive, and purposeful in their work with participants in the school community. However, principals are often quickly enculturated into behaviors that reinforce traditional expectations of dominance and patriarchy, all too often by teachers themselves. Teachers are among the most important forces in defining roles with and for administrators. Teachers outnumber principals, and many are older and more experienced than principals. Teachers give subtle and not-so-subtle messages to principals about their expectations. For instance, when teachers take action outside their classroom only when authorized, when they wait for permission to be innovators, they are signaling that an adult-to-adult relationship is not expected.

Principals, particularly early in their careers, can easily fall in line with these norms. When principals press for more adult and democratic relationships, they require the support of teachers in order to change the existing norms. When principals do not press for such norms, teachers can help define learning in the school community by being more explicit about their expectations.

In fact, a more assertive stance toward the relationship is needed on the part of both teachers and administrators. Teachers can enlist principals in being coconspirators in the work of school reform. They can reach out; invite conversations; orient new principals to the histories, cultures, and values of the school community; be explicit about their own needs, expectations, and visions. Often teachers are silent partners until problems occur or "permission" is needed. We are asking teachers to be active, vocal partners with principals—

taking vital responsibility for the enculturation of new administrators and the learning of veteran administrators.

The organizational policies and procedures of the district, of course, usually mandate the authority of the person in the principal's chair to carry out his or her established role. These uses of authority, however, are rarely successful without the collusion and cooperation of teachers. (See the discussion on power and authority in Chapter 6.)

Constructivist leadership provides the learning atmosphere in which individuals can collectively reframe their roles through continuous interaction and feedback from each other. Such leadership engages the reciprocal learning processes among us, reshaping our relationships and forming communities of learners and leaders.

Conclusion

Consider the story of Chavez Elementary and the homework problem. When Maria asks, "Why don't we challenge ourselves to think differently about this problem?" the silent faculty room was an all too familiar sound. If John hadn't asked, "Tell us what you mean, Maria?" her question would have faded into the air, followed by an unrelated comment. But he did ask the question, and the attention of the group changed. Both Maria and John performed significant acts of leadership.

As we have discussed, the teacher as constructivist leader is one who facilitates the reciprocal learning processes among colleagues, parents, and children in a school community. These processes enable participants to construct meanings that lead toward a shared purpose of schooling. When teachers such as Maria and John ask the next question that moves us through stages of learning, a shift takes place in the development of the entire community and in the learning of each participant.

Leading is thoughtful and skillful work, and yet it is even more than that. To be able to engage in this work, a teacher must possess a perspective that is not usually a part of our preparation or experience as teachers. That perspective is systemic and ecological in nature.

In Chapter 3, we will build on the understandings of the essential quality of relationships and community that form the foundation of constructivist leadership and suggest that these elements exist within an ecological perspective governed by wholeness, interdependence, multiple relationships, and networks.

By "an ecological perspective," we mean an understanding of the relationships among people and their environments. These interdependent relationships characterize "living systems," systems that—like school communities—are continually learning.

Changing the System

A Prerequisite to Saving Our Schools

It is only by individuals taking action to alter
their own environments that there is any chance
for deep change. The "system" will not, indeed
cannot, do us any favours. If anything, the
educational system is killing itself because it is
more designed for the status quo while facing
societal expectations of major reform.

Michael Fullan, *Change Forces* (1993)

FACILITATING RECIPROCAL LEARNING PROCESSES
requires that a leader develop a perspective that encompasses the
whole school community. Making a difference among colleagues,
parents, and children requires leadership behaviors on the part of
teachers that Fullan (1993) describes as "being self-conscious about
the nature of change and the change process" (p. 12). Such a consciousness about change requires an understanding of the dynamics
of systems and of systems thinking. We are proposing that the work
involved in making a difference—and therefore these perspectives—
is central to the work of teachers who will lead the change in their
schools, classrooms, and profession.

One's capacity to influence the system requires the ability to understand the relationship of teachers and individual classrooms to
the larger educational system. In this chapter, we will discuss three

33

areas to assist teacher leaders in developing the abilities needed to make a difference in schooling: (a) thinking and acting ecologically, (b) understanding organizational dynamics outside classrooms, and (c) working in concert with others to change the present system.

The Present System

At the present time, many teachers see themselves as being at or near the bottom of a hierarchical order in school districts. Shedd and Bacharach (1991) describe three existing models of educational systems: the factory management model, the bureaucratic model, and the craft workshop model. Each of those models is based on a set of assumptions about the purpose of schooling, about the nature of teaching, and about students (pp. 52-59). Interestingly, all three models are hierarchical; all share the assumption that knowledge and authority to make systemic decisions reside at the top.

Modern bureaucratic or hierarchical thinking is derived from 17th-century Western images designed by Newton and Descartes of the universe as mechanistic and hierarchical. Margaret Wheatley (1995a) described the origins of present organizations in the following way:

> We have believed not only that the world was like a great clock that some clockmaker had set in motion and then left, but also that we ourselves were machines. Unfortunately, this is still the dominant view in most schools. But machines do not have self-motivation; machines can't learn; machines have no intelligence. (p. 1)

Machine-like hierarchical systems are designed to preserve the status quo. The conditions for self-motivation, learning, and development of intelligence are not fostered there because these factors would surely challenge the status quo. Given our belief that schools need to change and that teachers are the people best situated to drive that change, we propose a different model for schools—one that is characterized by a nonhierarchical kind of thinking. We call this an ecological model of school organization—one that recognizes and builds on the relationship between people and their environments.

In an ecological model, people think and act systemically. Let us explain.

Thinking and Acting Ecologically

Recently, organizational theorists have begun to draw on ecological theory that is derived from an understanding of living systems in our environment. These understandings are assisting us in the design of organizations. We submit that the "ecological paradigm" is in tune with designing human systems for several reasons. As human beings, we are actually part of the earth's living system. We can readily draw on the knowledge of healthy living systems on this earth to guide the design of our social systems.

Think of a redwood forest, a desert, or an Arctic tundra. From the smallest bacteria to the largest plants and animals, diverse organisms and multiple species live together and are affected by water, sun, heat, cold, chemicals, seasons, and new species. This is an ecological system. One could use a similar frame of reference for thinking about the school and the classroom. These are places where children and adults are together, where their existence and patterns of relationships are affected by the school building, the resources allocated to the school, the economy of the community, the various cultures within it, the influence of new arrivals, new laws, state or university requirements, and so on.

There are natural scientists and social scientists who are ready to assist educators in making further comparisons to gain deeper understanding of the dynamics of living systems. Fritjof Capra (1995) traces the changes of thinking in science from traditional, mechanistic forms to living systems or ecological thinking (Tables 3.1 and 3.2, to come later, will explain these changes in thinking). He describes these shifts in several ways. Among them are the shift

- from mechanistic to ecological,
- from focusing on parts to considering the whole,
- from focus on objects to focus on multiple relationships,
- from hierarchies to networks as basic structures, and
- from competition among species to partnerships in the environment.

The mechanistic view is based on several beliefs and assumptions that we find problematic when thinking about how a social system like a school might change. For example, the mechanistic view of the system relies on external experts and assumes little internal capacity for knowledge or capabilities. In this view, individual objects are parts, operating independently. Competition to secure resources, rather than cooperation for sharing them, is the norm.

The ecological perspective, on the other hand, looks at the whole system rather than focusing on individual parts. This leads to discovering that multiple relationships are important for sustaining life; interdependence is the rule. These interdependent relationships occur through multiple networks. They are not hierarchies. They represent partnerships more than competition. The ecological perspective assumes that the organization innately has the resources and internal capacity to adapt and evolve in response to the environment.

In the school and classroom context, we assume that adults and children collectively possess resources and capacities to learn, adapt, and evolve in response to changing conditions. These conditions include changing knowledge about learning and specific discipline areas, changing school populations, changes in governance, and additions or reductions in resources (including people's time as well as financial support).

The internal capacity to self-organize in response to changing conditions enables an organization to be self-renewing. The idea of "self-organization" is gaining prominence in both schooling and business because it elegantly describes what we observe happening in settings in which change is beginning to take hold. In science, self-organization means that as a living system becomes more complex, it begins to spontaneously reorganize itself into more effective ways of working.

What does becoming "more complex" look like in schools? The more people participate in the work of leadership toward common purposes and goals, the more dense the relationships become and the more complex the school environment becomes. Teachers begin to suggest other ways of getting their most important work done: study groups, ad hoc committees, peer planning or coaching, teams, action research groups. This process of reorganizing the work of the school is what we think of as self-organization. We will frequently return to this idea in this book.

Clearly, a school that is self-organizing has more capacity for self-renewal; that is, it is continually improving itself. "A self-renewing system," points out Wheatley, "becomes more efficient in the use of its resources and better able to exist within its environment" (1992, p. 92).

Table 3.1 more fully describes the differences between the traditional, hierarchical thinking that we have experienced, and still continue to experience, and ecological thinking. This table represents the shift in scientific thinking in the Western world. The Descartes-Newtonian (mechanistic) model dominated how people in Western Europe and the United States understood the organization of nature. It followed that many of those principles would be used in forming our organizations and institutions as hierarchies and bureaucracies.

Although this current adjustment in thinking by Western scientists, sociologists, anthropologists, and psychologists represents a major paradigm shift of the fundamental belief system that dominates how we organize ourselves in society, ecological thinking has long been present in other parts of the world in nondominant cultures. Indigenous people in many cultures have lived according to ecological principles for thousands or even millions of years.

We can use ecological principles to begin making comparisons of the characteristics of most of our present educational systems to features in systems dominated by ecological design principles. Table 3.2 provides a framework for describing these shifts. The following section provides specific examples from school life.

Comparing Bureaucracies to Ecologically Designed School Systems

We have often thought of leadership in hierarchies as involving leaders and followers—those ahead and those following behind. Networks, on the other hand, function most effectively when many people are assuming leadership roles and responsibility in service of the network's purpose. Two examples comes to mind. A small network of a teacher, a student, and her parent comes together to examine that student's performance and work in school. Information is exchanged and meaning is constructed as the members of this little network give and receive feedback from one another in this context. This reciprocal exchange (giving and receiving) makes this a

TABLE 3.1 The Shifts From Hierarchical and Bureaucratic
                 Thinking to Ecological Thinking

Traditional Principle and Its Underlying Beliefs	*Common Ecological Principle and Its Roots in Current Scientific Thinking*
From Parts: Organisms are viewed as separate parts, independent of one another in the environment. Relationships between species are linear (e.g., the food chain). The environment is seen as separate from rather than connected to organisms.	**To Whole:** Focus is on the whole community and the interdependence within it. Multiple species contribute shelter, food, energy, and matter to the environment for one another. For example, feeding relationships are now described as food cycles with many interconnections (food webs) rather than as food chains.
From Objects: Reality is seen as existing in objects—those forms or substances that can be weighed and measured.	**To Relationships:** Reality consists of multiple relationships between the many parts of the environment that keep it living. To analyze and understand these relationships, their patterns must be mapped.
From Hierarchies: Describes species in the environment in hierarchical terms: higher and lower order. This infers that capabilities for learning and dominance belong in the higher-order beings.	**To Networks:** These are the patterns that describe the relationships within and between species. Information, energy, and matter flow along these lines of connections, creating feedback loops. These loops allow organisms to self-correct, self-regulate, and ultimately, self-organize. Every living community is a learning community.
From Competition: Early Darwinists saw organisms in competition with one another for food. Organisms within and among species were viewed as struggling for survival: "Survival of the fittest."	**To Partnership:** Twentieth-century scientists have learned that cooperation is the dominant mode of operating in an ecosystem. Interdependence and self-organization form a collective, not competitive, enterprise.

NOTE: The material in this table is drawn from dialogue sessions with Fritjof Capra and others at the Center for Ecoliteracy, Berkeley, California, as well as from his writing (Capra, 1995).

TABLE 3.2 Comparison of Bureaucratic System With Ecological System

Mechanistic View	*Ecological View*
Hierarchies: School site staff members see themselves as dependent on district governance and hierarchy; district on state; state departments of education on legislature; and so on. Information is selectively shared and managed for various levels of the hierarchy as well as for public consumption. Meaningful feedback loops are rare or nonexistent on a formal basis within the system.	**Networks:** These are the patterns that describe the relationships within and among partners and role groups throughout the system. Information, energy, and resources flow along these lines of connection, creating feedback loops, and increasing shared understanding and meaning. These loops allow educational systems to self-correct, self-regulate, learn, and ultimately, self-organize. Every school community is a learning community; everyone shares leadership in sustaining and feeding the networks in the system.
Parts: Classrooms and school sites are viewed as separate entities, run by credentialed educators. Relationships with parents and community are infrequent and distant. Students are separated into categories, depending on individual differences. Communication is highly structured and infrequent among members within the school or between the school and its community.	**Whole:** The focus is on the whole community and the diversity and interdependence within it. People from various role groups, who have a stake in the system, contribute to the care, needs, and purposes of the system. Relationships between institutional units are described with many interconnections. Individuals in various roles prepare for and assume leadership in different ways at different times to serve the common shared purpose of the system.
Focus on Objects: Reality is seen as existing in forms and substances that can be weighed and measured. The student is considered the object of teaching. Learning is that which is measured by test scores and grades.	**Multiple Relationships:** Relationships and connections among the many parties (including students) who are engaged in the common purposes of education are valued and attended to. Relationships and the quality of

(continued)

TABLE 3.2 (Continued)

Mechanistic View	Ecological View
	connections between people are revealed through mapping, not through a preset model. Time and opportunity are allocated for these relationships to develop within the process of self-organization and learning and shared accountability.
Competition: Teachers and administrators distrust information and decisions made about the distribution of resources and recognition. Teaching is viewed as a private activity. Teachers tend to protect their areas of expertise and curriculum; resources are jealously guarded. Recognition of individual effort is sparse. Recognition of collective effort is given in a general, nonspecific manner.	**Partnership:** A sense of shared common purpose determines decisions regarding distribution of resources, allocation of time, leadership roles, and responsibilities. Recognition of effort, learning, and achievement is frequent and ongoing; it takes place as part of the process of self-organization and collective learning.

feedback loop, making it possible for each member in the network to make future changes in relation to the information and meaning that was gained.

Another example is teacher networks formed to study and examine school or student data, solicit feedback on practice, and derive meanings that will be incorporated into their work at their school or classroom site. Such networks may exist among teachers at one site or among different schools. They may focus on whole school change or on teaching in a specific discipline area. Teacher-developed knowledge about the teaching, learning, and schooling process, the change process, student assessment, and other topics related to effective development of programs for children are a largely untapped resource. Such networks, described further in following chapters, can be sources of information and feedback for the system within the school and within the district.

In both examples, the feedback must be authentic and members of networks must be receptive and open listeners if the process is to support reciprocal learning. Later in this chapter, we will discuss these issues of staff and school culture in greater detail.

Most schools function as a set of individual parts—classrooms—operating in isolation from one another. Teachers who work in this type of setting are prone to feel victimized by changing circumstances because the need for certainty is high. They often feel powerless in the system. Factors from outside the classroom (e.g., reduced or increased enrollment and resources, rumors of changing conditions, district assessment processes, political factions in the community) affect the teaching and learning process by increasing uncertainty and threat. When teachers feel isolated and victimized by the circumstances under which they work, negative emotions drain their energies for wholeheartedly participating in working with their students. Teachers who participate in whole school planning and decision making, who conduct inquiries into changing conditions for their schools and classrooms, and who feel membership in the whole school also have access to information that helps them to understand and participate in the system context. Rather than feeling victimized and drained, individuals with a broader perspective are more able to take a long-range view and separate facts from mere possibilities. Contributing one's voice to the work of the whole school strengthens the school's ability to meet its goals and can be personally satisfying as well.

For some time, teachers have been frustrated by accountability practices that treat student learning and performance as objects that can be measured by standardized instruments. Tests often leave out large chunks of knowledge, attitudes, and abilities that students will need to be successful in life. Many tests that claim to report school accountability do not provide information that helps the school to determine its own progress. Portfolios, containing student work over a longer period of time, reveal more than a yearly test that treats student learning as an object, a body of knowledge that can be weighed and measured. Through a portfolio, we can learn about a student's relationships in school to learning and subject matter: what that student has learned, what the rate of progress has been, where the special talents reside, and what needs exist are more fully displayed.

An effective way of understanding a school's progress toward school renewal is an examination of the multiple relationships and linkages in a school that are creating the leadership density we spoke of earlier. Mapping processes, where actual visual maps are drawn to reveal linkages and relationships in a school, can do a great deal to reveal problems and possibilities in school improvement. Several formats and templates for mapping relationships and planning have been developed for use in schools (Bailey, 1995b).

Competition without regard to the value of partnership is often the norm in bureaucracies. This can be destructive and debilitating to the organization's effective use of resources and to learning. Traditional relationships among the various levels of schooling (elementary, middle grades, high school) are competitive in the sense that each plays the "blame game" toward the other. "If only the elementary schools had done their job, ours wouldn't be so hard." Or "If only we didn't have to get these kids ready for high school . . . [we could do what we think would be best]." If teachers from the various levels were to join in partnership to conduct action research on topics of common importance (self-organization), issues of curriculum articulation and development could be accomplished at the same time as professional learning.

Working within networks with others and maintaining feedback loops among the participants in the networks require that leaders be able to take a broad view of the system. That view includes understanding a variety of perspectives and forming multiple relationships where collective meaning can be created. Partnerships in which individual and collective learning is supported can be formed in and among schools to work toward a shared purpose.

Additional Ecological Principles

When we begin imagining how ecology and ecological principles might guide our thinking in education, the principle of self-organization provides a good starting point.

SELF-ORGANIZATION

Margaret Wheatley (1995b) describes three domains of self-organization: information, relationships, and self-reference (p. 6).

These domains relate to one another as three overlapping circles, as in a Venn diagram.

Information and the sharing of information throughout the school are nourishment for an environment and necessary for self-renewal. Information is not hoarded or managed for fear that it may get into the wrong hands. Teachers, administrators, students, parents, and members of the broader community have access to information that has meaning to them and that is necessary for carrying out their role in the system.

Relationships are important because everyone needs to have access to everyone in the system. (See our extensive discussion of relationships in the previous chapter.) Relationships form a dense network of connections thereby increasing the complexity of the system and increasing the capacity for self-organization.

As these multiple relationships are formed, we become conscious of the multiple views and opinions we hold. Our perceptions are shaped by our beliefs and expectations. Teacher leaders, together with others, must consciously evoke potential in others in order to examine their basic beliefs about people, especially one another. In a system such as a school where multiple relationships are being formed, inquiry into assumptions that undergird our perceptions and knowledge help to strengthen the collective ability of the staff to self-organize and become self-renewing. Establishing whether people act primarily out of self-interest or seek community is a good place to start. If we hold unquestioned beliefs that people act only for individual gain, we are not as likely to share information along such networks.

This book is based on the belief that all members of schools need community to maintain resiliency and sustain life. This belief is supported through multiple research studies now available that link student learning achievement, engagement in school and with community, and prosocial development to meaningful and supportive relationships and to membership in community (Battistich et al., & Schaps, 1995; Comer, 1980; Fraser, 1991; Lipsitz, 1984; Wehlage, Rutter, Smith, Lesko, & Fernandez, 1990). Among the most striking research is in the area of resiliency in children. In this context, *resiliency* means that children are able to become productive, contributing members of society despite adverse conditions. Four conditions seem central to this capability:

1. Social networking, so that children feel connected to a network of relationships; at least one person cares deeply for them.
2. Meaningful work involving service to others, often through community work; children feel that their work matters to someone.
3. A sense of future and a role in determining that future; children need to learn goal-setting and planning skills.
4. Problem solving of the tough issues that confront them; children need to learn problem-solving strategies.

Relationships seem to be the basis of resiliency in humans, other living systems, and in social systems as well.

Self-reference refers to the sense of identity (who are we?) of the organization. In schools, cocreation of collective identity is a continuous process. Talking about who we are, what we represent to the community, and what our values and purposes are can be particularly powerful as a means of orienting new teachers to a school. Self-conscious attention to identity includes inquiring into questions like, Is what we are doing addressing what we intend to bring about? If not, what? And how? Such questions can be addressed only when the community examines data and evidence resulting from a school's work. This is an ongoing process and is built into every occasion when assessing student work, developing and revising curriculum, evaluating teacher performance, and examining schoolwide results.

Our individual and collective identities (our perspectives of who we are, our passions, talents, sense of purpose, and creativity) are vital elements in the creation of self-organizing systems. Our understanding of who we are becomes the basis for collectively organizing to realize the purposes and goals we are established to achieve. Changing the system requires that teachers maintain a long-term perspective rather than thinking and planning solely for short-term results. What teachers do today does influence what those students and teachers in the future have to build on. We are building futures for the present generation as well as many to come. Wheatley's domains for self-organization can assist us to understand and apply deep systemic change in our schools. As schools strengthen their uses of information, relationships, and identity, they become capable of responding to changing circumstances in the school environment and the society. The school becomes self-renewing and capable of sustaining life in a healthy functional manner.

In Capra's (1995) terms, this condition is called "sustainability." Sustainability is long-term commitment and adherence to improvement. As we noted in our discussion of authentic relationships, we are in there for the long haul. And we are capable of sustaining a vibrant, self-renewing system.

Capra (1995) highlights three more principles of ecological thinking that can assist us in designing healthy educational systems: flexibility, diversity, and coevolution.

FLEXIBILITY

Because our environments are changing all the time, flexibility is present in living systems all the time. The greater the ability of a system to fluctuate, the greater the adaptability of a living system. The power of flexibility enables self-organization to take place on a continuous basis. "The more variables are kept fluctuating, the more dynamic is the system, the greater flexibility, the greater is the ability to adapt to changing environmental conditions" (Capra, 1995, p. 7). We described some of the conditions and changes in our environment in Chapter 1. These context factors have the potential for stimulating change, although that has not always been the case.

In a self-organizing system, created and connected through dense networks, information feedback fluctuates because the environment is changing all the time. In such a state of flux, it has been common for those involved to try to maintain their balance, their equilibrium, and the status quo. Jeffrey Goldstein (1994) describes how an organization in a mechanistic system is drawn toward a state of equilibrium, maintaining the status quo. We seek to protect ourselves from being "done to" or manipulated to do something we don't understand, he explains. In contrast, in self-organizing systems, Goldstein reports that "the tendency to change and develop is inherent in the system's very possibilities; therefore, resistance to change does not need an external force to get it moving, as in the donkey model of change" (p. 68). Not only does the "donkey model of change," with its carrot-and-stick approach, not work, it actually creates resistance to change. By installing "carrots," such as merit pay for teachers and grades for students, or "sticks," such as evaluations focused on prescribed behavior rather than revealed results, our system sets up conditions that create cultural, political, and technical problems. These problems contribute to collective resistance to change because when people feel they are being manipulated, they choose to maintain the status quo.

If we are serious about developing the capacity for continuous change for the benefit of the students and society, then we need to seek approaches that do not create resistance. Learning and change can be natural forces in the continuing evolution of the human system. Collective resistance to change is reduced or nonexistent in self-organized systems because the network of relationships provides for the flow of information and communication as changes are occurring. A sense of collective identity keeps members connected with their central purpose. A strong sense of community with supportive and caring relationships among members can provide a sense of security—rather than resistance—in a changing environment.

DIVERSITY

Connection and relationships among diverse elements in the community are among the most important strategies of ecosystems and of life in general. In human communities, when subgroups are isolated, information does not get to them or from them back to the network. Diversity in this case results in friction, prejudice, and violence. It is not an advantage.

By comparison, in dense, complex, well-connected networks, those divisions are less likely. If a particular individual (such as a principal) leaves, the network can perform similar tasks. Students, issues, and ideas that matter do not fall through the cracks because responsibility for leadership is allocated among many people, focused on a common purpose and set of goals. Because people are connected with one another, differences become a strength rather than a liability.

Vibrant networks including groups of people from various backgrounds and points of view can develop multiple perspectives and strategies for solving problems. Dee Hock (1995), founder and CEO Emeritus of VISA USA and VISA International, describes such a system as "chaord," a word crafted to bring together chaos and order. He tells the story of the creation of the VISA system, which began with a single assumption and a single question: If there were no constraints whatever, if anything imaginable was possible, what would be the nature, not the structure, of an ideal organization to create the world's premier device for the exchange of value? Out of this question, five principles emerged (pp. 6-7):

1. The organization must be equitably owned by all participants.
2. Power and function must be distributive to the maximum degree.
3. Governance must be distributive.
4. The organization must be infinitely malleable yet extremely durable.
5. The organization must embrace diversity and change.

The story of the creation of the VISA system is a fascinating one that can inform us about high-functioning, self-organizing systems. As a society, we possess a wealth of various talents, abilities, and interests influenced by diverse cultures and ethnicity. We are preparing future generations to participate effectively in a worldwide economy, in our country's democracy, and in maintaining a healthy environment that sustains life; therefore, we need to draw on all aspects of our diversity. This richness will enable us to solve hard social and economic problems and create a sustainable future. For example, Native American culture is embedded with understandings and wisdom about creating and maintaining healthy, ecological systems. In ecological systems, then, diversity is seen as an important asset. Working to enhance this asset by developing networks of strong relationships is essential.

COEVOLUTION

As the environment and society continue to change, professional educators, parents, students, and community members in partnership continue to know one another better. In the necessary exchange of information that characterizes all conversations, systems coevolve: They learn and change in concert with one another. One organism within the system influences another.

Conversely, in a hierarchical model, the "top" of the system controls, or attempts to control, the "bottom." Our reform history for the past 20 years demonstrates that this system of top-down control need not be the case. As described by the ecological principle of co-evolution, one organism within an environment influences another but does not control it. Even in our present system, we can see this principle play out; the school district policies influence what happens in schools and classrooms but do not control them.

Reform that improves learning in schools will not occur without the exchange of information, energy, and resources among all the entities within the educational system. Using ecological principles to redesign educational systems (classrooms, schools, districts, institutions, and agencies that support student learning and families) will help build sustainable futures for our children. A sense of community, important for the learning and well-being of students and those who work with them, is necessary in an ecologically designed system. Mechanistic structures do not provide for community; they do not support the self-organization of human talents and energies; in fact, they create resistance to change.

We propose, therefore, that we begin this complex move toward change by replacing our assumptions about how schools run from a hierarchical, mechanistic model characterized by top-down authority and control to a more ecological model characterized by interdependence and networks. In Chapter 6, we will look more closely at issues of power, authority, and control. In the next section, we will begin to consider how to connect this ecological thinking with the functions of school organizations as we know them.

Thinking Ecologically and Understanding Organizational Dynamics

Teacher leaders will need to join together to take the first steps toward designing the ecological conditions described above. One of the first tasks will be to think organizationally about agendas and activities to consider alternative approaches for change. One starting place might be to consider how ecological thinking and action can begin to take the place of old structures. We will review the issue of structures in the next chapter when we propose guidelines for developing structures for learning communities.

Mary Catherine Bateson, in *Peripheral Visions* (1994), tells of research she conducted to discover how people learn language and culture. At a time when she was caring for her own infant daughter, she studied mothers and infants and began to understand that "participation precedes learning" (p. 41). Lev Vygotsky (1962), as noted in Chapter 2, concluded that learning, or sense making, in cultural development followed interaction between people. If teachers use ecological principles to guide their collective participation in their school systems and if they lead the effort to reflect and converse together to construct their learning, then creating the leadership capacity for changing the system becomes part of the shared work. And as Michael Fullan (1993) concludes, "It is only by individuals taking action to alter their own environments that there is any chance for deep change" (p. 40).

Constructivist leadership for teachers requires the ability to apply the design principles and images we are describing to the dailiness of school life—to participate in changing without an expectation of perfection or full understanding of the process. If learning follows from participation, a measure of success is the constructivist process itself whereby both the organization and its participants are constantly evolving. These processes take time yet yield significant learnings throughout the process.

In the following section, we will propose a guide for thinking about and planning for participation in evolutionary change. Action in these areas includes raising questions, taking action, and connecting with others who share a sense of purpose. In this way, teacher leaders can bridge from where schools are now to a school that better meets the needs of students, teachers, administrators, parents, and community members. A school that meets the needs of its inhabitants can be sustainable in a life-giving way.

Thinking Organizationally, Starting With the School

Four areas of focus for whole school change are portrayed in Figure 3.1. *Whole school* is a view that sees the school as an organiza-

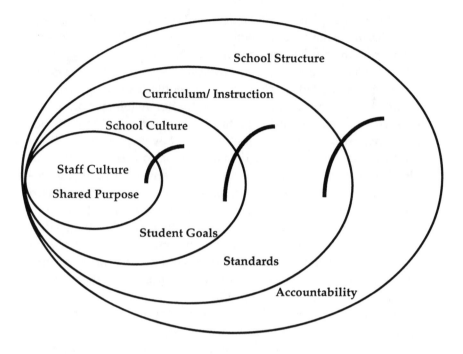

Figure 3.1. Areas of Focus for Organizational Change and Learning

tion made of many parts that are all connected to influence a student's daily, weekly, yearly educational experience. Any one of these areas may be used as a starting point for focusing change agendas, but ultimately, all four will need to be addressed, sometimes simultaneously.

No one individual or group, acting alone, can change a school. This is a beginning premise for our discussion. Similarly, making changes within an organization in isolation from others is nearly impossible. Connecting with organizations and individuals in the environment who have a stake in students' education is essential. The first order of business, therefore, is to gather together with others to examine the school community's ecological strengths and weaknesses. This gathering must plan to engage the entire school community in the school change process.

Teaching and leading are complex activities and cannot be "formula driven." Changing the system is complex as well. The areas outlined below provide a starting point for changing the school organization.

STAFF CULTURE AND SHARED COMMON PURPOSE

At the core of school change agenda is staff culture, which is composed of the norms, beliefs, and values that constitute the way things are done in a particular school setting. Understanding this culture is the prerequisite condition for the development of learning communities.

The term *staff* refers to the people who call the school their place of work. The nature of relationships among the staff members sets the tone for the school. Students are more likely to be motivated and engaged in schools where the staff is energetic and positive, shares goals, and openly demonstrates their care for others (Anderman & Maehr, 1994; McLaughlin & Talbert, 1992). Among elements that make up staff culture are beliefs about

- one another,
- the way the staff works together (or doesn't),
- students,
- the community, and
- the fundamental purpose of the school.

These beliefs are shared among staff members and are often operating unconsciously.[1] People new to the staff are most likely aware of elements of staff culture when they encounter the socialization process.

In her studies of over 70 elementary schools, Susan Rosenholz (1989) found differences in staff cultures, characterizing them as "moving" or "stuck." In staff cultures operating with norms of collegiality and in "moving" (as opposed to "stuck") cultures, teachers value learning together. In studies of high schools and high school department cultures, Milbray McLaughlin and Joan Talbert (1992) found some groups operating with norms of isolation and some with norms of collegiality.

In both the Rosenholz and the McLaughlin/Talbert studies, the researchers found positive effects for students in moving or collegial cultures. Their research reveals that a staff culture that supports in-depth collaboration, a willingness to confront old assumptions, and an openness to discuss hard issues lead to schoolwide or department-mentwide changes that benefit students and their learning. Connecting, relating, and learning together do make good conditions for student engagement and learning in school.

Staff culture is created through experiences that take place over time. Effects of those experiences sometimes impose habits of organization, behavior, and relationship that, once relevant to the situation, are no longer appropriate. School schedules provide an example. Operating on a school year that allocates 2 ½ months vacation in the summer, schools still function to support an agrarian economy based on the need to have children at home during harvest time. Despite our changed economy, we continue the practice. When this schedule is challenged, respondents say, "But we've always done it this way."

Staff culture can actually stand in the way of shared decision making. For example, staffs that are combined when a school is closed may experience difficulties coming to consensus over organizational issues. What they often do not realize is that this difficulty is not because of the issue itself but because staff culture issues were never brought to light. Suzanne Bailey (1995a) tells of an elementary school where the staff came to an impasse about the format of student report cards.

> They were divided into two camps—half for narrative report cards and half supporting the graded report cards they were currently using. Unable to resolve the conflict, which seemed to be both deepening and escalating, the principal sought help. During interviews with the principal and key staff members, other issues began to emerge. Some of these issues had been revisited often and had long histories. The consultant discovered that there was a division between veteran staff and newcomers. (p. 21)

In this case, the staff created a *histomap*, a visual representation of that school's history.

> Several patterns emerged in the dialogue: the lack of inte-
> grating two staffs into one after a school closing and the rift
> that marked all future interaction; the need to publicly ac-
> knowledge and grieve the death of a previous principal
> whose memory prevented new principals . . . from [becom-
> ing] active leaders at the school; the total decline of parent
> and community involvement—coffees, suppers, Saturday
> Fairs—that had been the "drivers" of successful school im-
> provement initiatives. (p. 21)

As a result of this dialogue and how it functioned to bring uncon-
scious material into the collective consciousness of the group, they
mobilized to take action together, both within the school staff and in
conversations with parents and students, to focus on the future. Creating together a visual histomap or "journeymap" of the history of
the school can help staff members become conscious of factors in
their culture that are affecting the way they work together. This strategy helps a group to evoke potential—beliefs, assumptions, and perceptions—the first phase of constructivist learning.

If norms of collegiality already exist, and teachers assume that
working and learning together is a necessary feature of success for
their students and for themselves, then such a map gives the group,
collectively, a basis for conversations and dialogue on how to build
on that base. In staffs where a culture that supports collective learning does not exist, it is advantageous to develop and commit to a collective vision of a staff culture that would support excellence in work.

Creation of a staff's cultural vision that includes developing
norms that will support staff members' sense of efficacy is one of
several processes that support whole school reform. In using such a
process, Karen Kent and Rich Gemmet (1990-1995) found a pattern
of common themes emerging across most of the 50 schools they
worked with. Some of these themes are remarkably similar to those
identified by researchers as norms for collegial cultures:

- Open, honest communication, including expressing disagree-
  ments
- Respect for one another
- A unified focus on students or student learning
- Cooperation or collaboration with one another[2]

It is as though school staffs intuitively know what Rosenholz, Little, Glickman, McLaughlin and Talbert, and others have found in their research on collegial staff cultures. These researchers also learned that shared purpose, or we could say a common sense of identity, and commitment to work and learn together, are necessary attributes for achieving excellence in education in today's world. Those norms also reflect the importance of relationships among staff members linked together with a sense of purpose that connects them with students and student learning.

When a school staff determines a need for a more supportive culture and has created a vision of how they want to work in relationship with one another, occasions and rituals to mark a new beginning are useful vehicles for moving the change process forward. Two teacher researchers, Ann Gessert-Wigfield and Alan Vann Gardner (in press), developed a case study of their school's process in reframing their experiences through changes in assumptions about responsibility, leadership, and voice and to help this staff make sense of their new lives together. They noted the significance of such an occasion:

> As a part of beginning anew, we planned a ritual for parting with the old. We gathered by the creek, made a fire, and burned years and years of old chart papers with goals, strategic plans, etc. This ritual symbolized a letting go of our old ways of going about our business—meeting upon meeting with little change and grade-level teams addressing their particular needs with little regard for overall school concerns. (p. 15)

Collaborative staffs need an overarching sense of common purpose to move toward better conditions for learning. Sharing a group sense of common purpose facilitates the group in determining priorities on the working and learning agendas. Sharing and connecting individual purposes, passions, and interests provide energy for connecting linkages among the staff members. These connections, and the accompanying collective energy, provide the fuel for the engine of change. They also create resiliency for the whole staff to reach out and establish meaningful connections with those in their environment. One can pose this question: If we were not organized here together, what would not be accomplished? Sharing a sense of purpose helps a school staff to construct meaning about their work and builds the basis for constructivist leadership and therefore a learning community.

SCHOOL CULTURE AND DESIRED STUDENT GOALS

The culture of the whole school community includes students, parents, staff of community agencies and government, districtwide staff and members of boards of education, and (as available) university faculty. The attitudes, values, and beliefs of the people who reside in the community surrounding the school are critical information for teachers if they are to ensure student success in learning. It is essential to explore the multiple perspectives of community members about children, learning, and schooling.

The staff culture influences how the whole school culture develops. One example is contained in Suzanne Bailey's previous elementary school story. When the staff members were not connected with one another, parents and community members declined to be involved. When staff relationships were strong, connections with the school community were also active.

Figure 3.2 illustrates how a healthy school organization, with dense connections characterized by relationships that support the flow of information among the staff members, is connected with its environment, the broader community. There are multiple avenues for exchange of information, many opportunities for establishing relationships. Direct linkages between teachers and those in the community, the district, and the profession are acknowledged for their value to the whole school. The greater the density of the connections among the school staff, which is characterized by both conversations and dialogues that construct organizational learning as well as shared work, the greater the capacity to interact authentically with those in the environment. As we have noted, this condition leads to greater resilience to work with changes in the environment. Figure 3.2 illustrates this dynamic.

In an ecological sense, an organism must connect with its environment to access the matter and energy necessary for sustaining life.

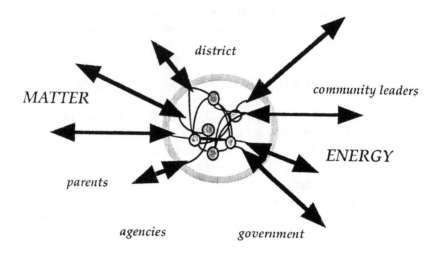

Figure 3.2. Exchange of Matter and Energy With the Environment

Sources of matter for school systems consist of money, materials, and peoples' time. Sources of energy might be vision and energy that others outside the school staff bring to supporting the school mission and to meeting the educational and social needs of students in the community. This energy can help to create a political climate that works for (or against) the goals of teaching and learning. In human systems, we are dependent on those sources of energy and we can nurture them through conscious, reciprocal, and authentic exchange of information.

Often, in the present notion of school, one person (usually the principal) holds sole responsibility for communicating and linking with others in the community and school district office. Meaning, diverse perspectives, and trust are bound to be lost when sole responsibility for holding the perspective of the whole school and for communication with the surrounding community resides with one person or a small group. A teacher in the Gessert-Wigfield and Vann Gardner (in press) case study previously cited reflected on the relationship between voice and trust: "The more individuals have a voice, the more that you find in common and what emerges are the highest qualities of relationship, like honesty." After analyzing numerous interviews, surveys, and observations of school meetings, these researchers concluded that

> The more people trust that their voice will be heard and the more a community voices and listens to each other's concerns, the deeper the relationships grow and the more effective their decisions and actions. Not only do people discover that which they share in common, but they feel safe to express diverse points of view. In such a model, resistance can be redefined as difference, and difference is a positive factor of growth. (p. 14)

A school staff will receive more honest feedback depending on the manner in which they reach out to others in the environment. The more honest the feedback and open the flow of information, the greater the capacity to organize for meeting changing needs. The staff and other community members need to look for patterns in the feedback that they receive. The density of this information can help to alleviate the tendency of vocal, but narrow, interest groups to dominate community influence on the system. And the more honest a staff can be in providing meaningful feedback and information to others in the environment, the greater the possibility of finding understanding of the school's goals and aspirations within the broader community.

In determining and refining goals for students, it is critically important to engage those who have a stake in students' education. Marvin Weisbord (1992) has developed strategies for bringing large groups of diverse stakeholders to an organization's work and planning. They engage together in finding their common ground for goal setting. Weisbord and others (Alban & Bunker, 1990) have documented instances in which 200 to 2,000 people can share such experiences. These occasions are excellent opportunities for setting a stage and for creating a set of common understandings.

Tom Abbey, a teacher researcher from a small junior/senior high school in California, describes his staff's process of engaging the community and students in articulating goals:

> Identifying a variety of stakeholders and beginning a dialogue helped us produce a catalog of skills, knowledge, and attitudes that we all believed any graduate of Calistoga ought to exhibit. We said, "If you'll help us determine the skills, knowledge, and attitudes, we'll create a curriculum that will deliver them."
>
> The stakeholders took us at our word, and their involvement was crucial as discussions about school change took place in the community. In the four years since then, those ideals have guided our school-wide discussions about change. (Kent & Abbey, 1995, p. 23)

The search for the common values shared by the diverse elements that make up the school culture and community is reflected in Abbey's comments. The conversations and dialogues among members who hold a stake in student learning are critical to discovering and describing goals and for learning from one another.

CURRICULUM, STANDARDS, AND INSTRUCTIONAL PRACTICES

The primary, and sometimes the sole, focus of reform efforts is most often curriculum, standards, and instructional practices. Reformers usually focus on individual classrooms, teachers, teaching, and needs of students. Although this approach appears to focus on what matters most, it tends to ignore the student's whole experience (daily, weekly, yearly, multiyear) of learning in school. In addition, factors in the whole school that influence the classroom, such as staff culture and the nature of connections with the school community, do not receive the attention they need. Conditions causing resistance to change are created when the sole focus is on individual teachers, who are usually practicing in isolation from colleagues. Teachers resist change when they experience feelings of being overwhelmed, confused, blamed, and unacknowledged.

On the other hand, past reform efforts *have* stimulated the development of new knowledge and practices about effective teaching and learning. This knowledge is available and accessible to teachers. The question is not, What is good curriculum and instructional practice? Rather, the questions now are: How do teachers use the knowledge of practice developed so far in their own contexts? and How does teachers' work contribute to the advancement of knowledge about teaching and learning?

It is important to remind ourselves that work on curriculum and instruction needs to address the school goals for students as well as curriculum standards. The manner in which teachers work together should be consistent with the staff's cultural vision and attentive to the school culture. Teacher leaders who are alert to these connections seek opportunities to engage others in attending to them. Professional practice relies on a continuous process of design, implementation, reflection, and revision among those working with the students.

SCHOOL STRUCTURES AND ACCOUNTABILITY TO STUDENTS AND PARENTS

The structures that are put in place for the use of time and resources, planning, and decision-making need to support the alignment of purpose and practices (e.g., school schedules, teaming arrangements, meetings and professional development, agreements with district offices, support providers outside the school). Teacher leaders seek opportunities to work with district offices and boards and employee unions to communicate the support they need to allocate time in the manner that supports the learning community for both school staff and students. Six guidelines for building learning community structures will be discussed in Chapter 4.

Assessment practices need to be data and performance based and relate to both student performance and school operation. Action research, conducted with a whole school focus, can provide opportunities for gathering data and reflecting on how the collective endeavors are progressing. Teacher and administrator researchers can analyze the effects of various practices on students, teachers, and parents, and what next steps are indicated for school change. Interviews, surveys, and focus group discussions, conducted on a regular basis among the broad community, allow the professional community to test assumptions and stay connected.

All this need not be the responsibility of teacher leaders alone. Morgan Lambert and Mary Gardner (1995) make a case for districts to create and manage information systems that "serve effectively to support informed decision-making, to build a culture of inquiry that is informed by data as well as driven by values" (p. 148). Teachers often do not trust such information gathered by school districts in a hierarchical, bureaucratic system, nor is it entrusted to teachers. In an ecologically designed system, the district is another organization in the environment, subject to similar flows of matter and energy and coevolving along with the schools serving the same community. District officials often see the perspective of the whole community and the connections among schools. That perspective can be a great advantage when considering a student's entire school experience. Teachers also need opportunities to step outside their own settings to explore other settings for learning more about themselves.

Fundamental Challenges

The first challenge for teacher leaders is changing our own perspectives of school. We are so trained in the thinking and language of mechanistic hierarchies that becoming conscious of our own assumptions will be critical to using an ecological paradigm. Because we use language in constructing knowledge, the use of more ecological, constructivist language, rather than mechanistic terms, is fundamental within the learning community.

> All views of the world are acquired, and learning a way of seeing the world offers both insight and blindness, usually at the same time. Losing the certainty of a particular world view can make you feel sick, bewildered, dizzy. From this point of view, culture shock is a withdrawal phenomenon; we reject the new because we have learned to be dependent on the old. In the same way, I may learn to trust someone, premising my life on that trust, and then be unable to reject it when I am betrayed. People will accept martyrdom in order to hold on to an idea. (Bateson, 1994, p. 91)

Bateson portrays the nature of one significant challenge for those teachers who step forward into leader roles. The nature of leadership in changing a system requires a person to be able to hold onto ideas, values, and beliefs and, at the same time, to hold those things in question. The nature of learning in community requires that leaders support and model the reciprocal processes of speaking one's mind and heart and listening when challenged. This is a very hard skill to master. As noted in Chapter 1, educators have been prepared for a profession that values certainty. If teachers are not viewed as experts, they sometimes feel as though they lose face. As Bateson points out, changing the culture might put an individual in a state of culture shock. Teachers who take on these roles find it necessary to develop personal practices that help them to maintain a sense of personal balance and flexibility, in addition to seeking relationships with others who also have taken up this challenge.

Advocating for changing the system can feel like unfamiliar territory and sometimes puts a teacher at odds with others. Here the challenge of clarity and courage comes into play—remaining open to others, not sacrificing oneself and one's beliefs just to get along. This courageous work goes better if the processes of inquiry, dialogue, and authentic conversation about differences and common ground become part of the learning practices within the school.

To respond to this first challenge, develop and sustain your own personal resources and commit to examining and challenging your own presumptions and actions that emerge out of bureaucratic, rule-bound traditions before you begin challenging others.

The second challenge is the challenge of power and control. Human systems differ from those we call "natural" systems in that we, as humans, use language, conceptual abilities, and culture as ways to interpret and understand the world we live in. Sometimes we use those capabilities to try to dominate one another rather than to influence and evolve reciprocally. When that occurs, issues of power and control emerge. Teacher leaders need to engage others in becoming conscious of their urges for control and dominance and to develop collegial practices for avoiding the use of power to serve their individual needs. This is a complex issue and will be discussed more fully in Chapter 6.

To begin responding to this challenge, engage others in learning about alternative systems and supporting one another in creating a professional

*culture for continuous learning. Engage with others in the school commu-
nity to create connections for ongoing reciprocal dialogue, feedback, and
learning.*

*The third challenge is the consideration of the whole school and its
relationship to all the parts that compose the educational system.* This will
require what David Orr (1994) calls "ecological design intelligence":

> [Ecological design intelligence] is the capacity to understand
> the ecological context in which humans live, to recognize
> limits, and to get the scale of things right. It is the ability to
> calibrate human purposes and natural constraints and to do
> so with grace and economy. At its heart, ecological design
> intelligence is motivated by an ethical view of the world and
> our obligations to it. On occasion it requires the good sense
> and moral energy to say no to things otherwise possible and,
> for some, profitable. The surest signs of ecological design
> intelligence are collective achievements: healthy, durable,
> resilient, just, and prosperous communities.
>
> Educators must become students of the ecologically pro-
> ficient mind and of the things that must be done to foster
> such minds. In time, this will mean nothing less than the
> redesign of education itself. (pp. 2-3)

Maria, at Chavez Elementary School described in Chapter 2,
challenged presumptions about homework. John, her colleague,
facilitated the process to examine assumptions more deeply. Both
teachers acted as constructivist leaders. Through these deceptively
simple acts, they were helping create a professional culture that values learning and connections for dialogue, feedback, and learning
through the faculty study groups. The teachers who gathered and
critically examined the data for implications for future work were
exercising leadership with a focus on a whole school issue.

Kent and Ellman (1990) describe the case of a beginning teacher
who was deeply disturbed by her inability to manage a classroom
that fit her images of teaching. A graduate of a developmental teacher
education program, her attention and energies were consumed by
working with and attending to 30 *individual* first graders. Her classroom was transformed when, six months into the school year, her
thinking opened up to what she called "waking up to my *group*."

When she realized that many individual needs would be better served by attending to the group norms and relationships, her teaching life became more satisfying, and the children performed better. Similarly, individual classroom needs will be better served if we attend to collective norms and relationships among the entire staff.

To respond to this challenge, seek opportunities to consider whole school conditions and actions as they relate to individual classroom teaching and point out ways that ecological design intelligence is enacted in your school.

Systemic change in our educational systems will occur when enough teachers, working together, summon the collective will to be proactive and persevere with courage toward common goals for better teaching and learning for adults and students. In our next chapter, we will explore in greater depth the substance and nature of the work, in community, for teachers learning and working together.

Notes

1. Edgar Schein (1992) has conducted in-depth studies in hierarchical organizations of staff culture. He defines culture, how it is created, how it evolves, and how it can be changed in corporate and other business settings in his book *Organizational Culture and Leadership.* This can be a helpful resource for those interested in pursuing existing research on organizational culture more deeply, realizing that such cultural dynamics may be different in ecologically designed educational settings.

2. These data were compiled by Karen Kent and Rich Gemmet in documenting their work in schools to build capacity for whole school change from 1990 to 1995. This work was part of the San Francisco Bay Region IV Professional Development Consortium program.

Constructing Understandings of Learning Communities

Essential Structures and Processes for Teacher Leadership and Systemic Change

Attempting to harness real change that is being pulled by intention, not pushed by prediction, is so complex that its understandings can only be constructed in the conversations among co-leaders in a learning community.

Lambert et al., *The Constructivist Leader* (1995)

WE DESCRIBED IN CHAPTER 1 SEVERAL CONTEXT clues affecting teaching and schooling. We argued that these context clues have "inherent power in defining who we are as teachers, the limits or boundaries imposed on our actions, and the futures that we perceive." We challenged teachers to work with themselves and others to alter the contexts of their professional lives. The context that we have been moving toward is one called a *learning community*.

In Chapters 2 and 3, we added a few additional concepts that pave a new road toward this learning community. Before going on, we'll briefly review the key ideas:

1. To lead is to facilitate the learning of adults and children in the community toward a common purpose.
2. To undertake the role of learning facilitator (leader) requires a rethinking of our roles as teachers as well as the roles of administrators and parents.
3. To understand how we move learners toward a common purpose, we need an "ecological" view—we must understand how the parts interact interdependently to form a whole.
4. The density of authentic relationships in a school determines its capacity for leadership and for diversity.
5. For learning communities to form, they must construct a sense of purpose and direction.

In this chapter, we will build on these ideas and describe what learning communities are, why they have been problematic, and how we build them in schools. We will provide some promising examples of work that engages educators in the building of learning communities.

What Is a Learning Community?

In thinking about defining a learning community, a familiar ancient Indian tale comes to mind: the tale of the blind men and the elephant. Each of the men tries to describe the elephant by approaching it from a different perspective. One climbs a ladder, touches the elephant's trunk, and says, "An elephant is long, thin, and round like a rope." Another touches the elephant's side and says, "An elephant is hard, smooth, and flat like a wall." Still another touches the elephant's leg and says, "An elephant is round, firm, and tall like a tree." All of them are correct in their assumptions, and yet none of them understands the elephant. If they were to combine their descriptions, they might have a sense of the features of the elephant; yet they would still be lacking the gestalt, the wholeness of the elephant. In learning communities, members must recognize their interdependence and view the community as a whole. This drive for wholeness creates a major tension in schools, because school community members often feel that their work is fragmented and incongruent. A sense of wholeness can focus the community on the collective purpose of the group and bring a feeling that life in school makes sense, that it has meaning.

Sometimes we refer to this collective understanding as *synergism*, where the results generated by the whole, acting together, are greater than the sum of individual efforts, acting separately. Living systems have *synergy*, energy that acts together. How does this occur?

Learning communities are the collections of self-organizing, learning circles that form when the learning processes among its participants involve a continual learning cycle. In Chapter 2, we described some of these processes as the "reciprocal processes" of leadership. A school must build into its daily routines opportunities for conversation in which participants surface assumptions, beliefs, memories, and perceptions (evoking potential). These conversations lead to exploration and inquiry: examining student work and school data, action research, visiting other schools, participating in networks (breaking set with old assumptions). The flow of this discovered information leads to conversations in which adults (and students, especially in secondary schools) reflect on, make sense of, and organize their thoughts (constructing meanings together). These learning processes evolve into plans for continuous improvement (reframing actions). A learning community involves a continual "wave" of conversation characterized by exploration, inquiry, construction of meaning, and action. Embedded in these processes is the development of relationships that grow in density as educators work collegially to unfold the learning cycle. This is the process of co-evolution in schools. It is constructivist learning.

According to Peter Senge (1990), a learning organization (community) is "a place where people continually expand their capacity to create the results they truly desire, where new and expansive patterns of thinking are nurtured, where collective aspiration is set free, and where people are continually learning how to learn together" (p. 14). We think of this capacity for collective actions and attitudes as leadership.

The concept of the cycle of learning has deep roots. In the 1940s, Kurt Lewin proposed the idea of action research as inquiry into practice. In the 1950s, Norbert Weiner developed *cybernetics* as a cycle of learning involving the feedback of information so that a process, group, or even machine could "self-correct"—that is, use information about how the process is working in order to improve its operation (or by analogy, using samples of student work to determine how the teaching and learning process is going). The conversations that developed these processes and eventually applied them to social organizations occurred in New York in the 1950s and 1960s and were known as the Macy conferences (Capra, in press).

The application of cybernetics to organizations emerged in business and schools from the "total quality movement," led by Deming (1982), in which establishing measures of evidence for determining movement toward identified goals became the focus for performance and decision making. Deming added a critical element, the full participation and involvement of all of the members of these organizations, and the learning organization came into clearer focus.

By the 1980s, education was valuing several strategies from other fields that converged with these notions, such as the cooperative involvement of all group members and the use of inquiry. At the classroom level, cooperative approaches were being substantially researched and were yielding impressive results. Approaches that valued both collective and individual learning were emerging, bringing forth a resurgence of ideas around active, engaged learning. At the same time, brain research and cognitive research were confirming what we had learned from Vygotsky decades before: that human interaction actually results in a growth in intelligence.

By the mid-1980s, Barth (1988) was writing about a "community of learners," and followers of Gregory Bateson (1972)—who, with Margaret Mead, had been at the Macy conferences—were using "ecological" notions about schools. These complementary movements forged the concept of the *learning community*. It was not until the 1990s, however, that further insight was gained into the use of the cycle of learning as it related to schools and how that process could propel the community, creating its energy, interdependence, and motion.

Why Are Learning Communities Problematic?

"Community building must become the heart of any school improvement effort. . . . It requires us to think community, believe in community, and practice community" (Sergiovanni, 1994, p. 95). Yet few schools are what we would describe as learning communities.

Instead of being focused, interdependent places for people to find meaning, they are often fragmented, separated places where purpose is difficult to find.

Learning communities are difficult to create. They require complex, authentic relationships that involve the whole person (all that we are—emotional, social, cognitive, and experiential). They require trust, infusion of new ideas, facilitation, time to honor reflection and learning, and respect for individual differences. Yet as difficult as it is, we seem to have an innate need for community. Sergiovanni (1994) argues that the desire for community is part of human nature: "We humans seek meaning and significance above all, and building purposeful communities helps us find both" (p. 98).

Why is the building of learning communities so problematic? Several reasons immediately appear in response to that question. Members of school communities are individuals—often individualists—with diverse philosophies, experiences, expertise, and personalities. They come to their work with varying values, skills, knowledge, and beliefs. Often they are the blind men with the elephant. On the one hand, we invite and value diversity; it contributes to the disequilibrium that generates energy for learning and for change. On the other hand, it presents a challenge in learning how to collaborate, to listen, to learn, and to respect the multiplicity of thinking in the school community. Diversity can be both a benefit and a concern, depending on the attitudes and commitment of individuals in the school community. As we noted in the last chapter, "connection and relationships among diverse elements in the community are among the most important strategies of ecosystems and of life in general. In human communities, when subgroups are isolated, information does not get to them or from them back to the network. Diversity in this case results in friction, prejudice, and violence. It is not an advantage." On the other hand, as we will consistently note, as relationships in schools become more dense, as community members listen to each other and learn together, diversity becomes an advantage.

If members of a school community have not experienced themselves as learners individually, they will not be able to help create learning for others. Learners must be willing to suspend assumptions, respect the ideas of others, and engage in dialogue, continually constructing their understandings. When members of a school community are not engaged in such learning, they may resent the introduction of new ideas and the implementation of innovations that disrupt their routines. In school systems where routines are honored and "turf" is guarded, it is difficult to encourage the collaboration that engages collective learning. And in schools and districts where learning is viewed as the annual mandated staff development training event and an evaluation checklist, the learning community that we envision seems like a distant illusion.

As we have noted in earlier chapters, in school systems in which authority and power are invested exclusively in the hierarchy, shared leadership is not welcomed. Teachers find security and protection in their individual classrooms, a small group of confidantes, and their lives outside of school. Teachers may not accept responsibility for the welfare of the whole, because wholeness is not a part of their lives.

These are daunting obstacles to the building of learning communities. The reader may wonder whether it is even possible—or whether it is worth the effort. Yet teachers as leaders are in a prime position to interrupt this process of sustaining practices, routines, behaviors, and attitudes that circumvent and block the flow of learning in the community. The bipolarization of thinking, self-oriented behaviors, and blaming of others for discouraging outcomes can begin to change as teachers assume leadership roles and take actions to examine and resolve some of the dysfunctions that maintain aspects of the system. They can, instead, facilitate a process of creating a learning community focused on a common purpose.

How Do We Build Learning Communities? The New Road Ahead

One of our assumptions in this book is that teachers must assume the major responsibility for saving our schools. At the heart of this responsibility is altering the context in which teaching and learning take place—building a learning community. In this next section, we will examine several aspects of the learning community—including teaching learning, taking leadership actions, and moving toward collegiality and collaboration. Furthermore, we will recommend structural changes in schools that are needed to establish such communities. In the comparison of characteristics of learning environments shown in Table 4.1, we can see the shift in behaviors and attitudes as

TABLE 4.1 A Shift in Thinking Toward Learning Communities

Traditional	Evolving
Strict adherence to traditional role of teacher as technician with specific standards to adhere to.	Pursuit of teacher as learner, leader, shaper, and innovator.
Professional development activities rely heavily on formalized staff training sessions.	Professional development activities are designed and identified by the learner and the community.
Teachers' interactions are limited and structured by hierarchical design (e.g., staff meetings, departmental grouping).	Teacher interactions are characterized as networks for flow of information systems and learning. They are encouraged and supported by the system.
Teacher evaluations adhere to peer standards established by others.	Teacher assessments lead to peer and self-assessments, encouraging feedback from their work.
Teachers' professional environment is dominated by valuing conformity, compliance, and standardization.	Teachers' professional environment is adaptable, challenging, and energized by innovation, learning, and valuing of community.

we move toward learning communities. The environmental shifts described in these comparisons call for building leadership capacity by involving more adults in their own learning and the learning of others. This entails collaboration and dialogue, listening and observing, and learning to become collegial.

Establishing Powerful Learning With Teachers

If we are to consider teachers as leaders in building community and facilitating learning for themselves and for others, what are their perceptions of what constitutes powerful learning? As we listen to teachers construct the attributes they consider to be key contributors to their learning, we can identify the connections between leadership actions and the features of a learning community.

Recently, in working with a group of 75 teacher center-leaders in the New York City Public Schools, Mary Dietz chose the following activity as a beginning point to facilitate the construction of the purpose, meaning, and function of a professional development portfolio (see pp. 83-85). She began by asking teachers to write a description of the most powerful professional learning experience they could recall. Keeping in mind that surfacing prior experience, perceptions, and beliefs is the first fundamental step in constructivism, she wanted to invite their current understanding of "learning" for themselves. After allowing for reflection time, she asked them to share their descriptions with a partner, and together they identified critical attributes that contributed to their powerful learning experiences. The groups' consolidated list of critical attributes of powerful learning included the following:

1. *Purposeful and focused learning* that addresses identified needs and interests of the learner
2. *Recognition of philosophy* invited by discussions about the meaning of one's work and shared beliefs
3. *Articulation of intentions* regarding personal purpose and meaning for learning
4. *Self-consciousness* or awareness of what one's work is
5. *Renewal* that comes from valuing one's work and the work of others
6. *Feedback and debriefing* sessions after observations and sharing
7. *Walking the talk,* opportunities to practice new ideas and make modifications over time
8. *Structures, organizers, and processes* to focus learning (e.g., action research and study groups)
9. *Collaborations* to build relationships and share diverse points of view
10. *Relevance* to learning opportunities and connections to one's work

Similar responses have been generated by subsequent groups of teachers as they reflect on their own learning. Relationships, awareness of what one is doing, and an interest in seeking new ideas are themes that constantly appear. Intentions and consciousness of the effectiveness of one's practices were critical factors. The consciousness and sharing of one's beliefs and practices is articulated, revealed, examined, and revised as teachers practice learning and leading together.

In *Stewardship* Peter Block (1993), comments, "If there is not transformation inside of us, all the structural change in the world will have no impact on our institutions" (p. 77). Before teachers can build a community based on learning, they must first view themselves and each other as learners. In Chapter 7, we will describe principles for a broadened view of professional learning and its rich intersection with leading.

Leadership Actions and Attitudes

To better understand our perspective on leadership actions, let's revisit the definition of constructivist leadership: "the reciprocal processes that enable participants in an educational community to construct meanings that lead toward a common purpose about schooling." If leadership is defined as a concept transcending individuals, roles, and behaviors, then anyone in the educational community—teachers, administrators, parents, students—can engage in leadership actions. Leadership actions represent reciprocal processes, participation in educational communities, and constructing a common meaning about the purpose of education. In other words, leadership is the participatory opportunities that exist among us in a school community and is characterized by collegial interactions among staff members.

The leadership actions that accompany this understanding of constructivist leadership reflect the theoretical foundation of constructivist learning theory. These are actions and environmental attributes that support and develop teachers as constructivist leaders. If our schools are to be learning communities, centers, or homes for making meaning, we must consider the acts of leadership that enable learning communities to evolve. These acts involve the following:

> *A sense of purpose and ethics* because explicit values, honesty, and trust are fundamental to relationships. Teachers as leaders must be highly regarded and respected for who they are as people if they are to gain credibility and authority as colleagues and leaders.

Facilitation skills are necessary, because framing, deepening, and moving the conversations about teaching and learning are fundamental to constructing meaning. Teachers as leaders introduce and model effective facilitation skills in assisting the community in the reciprocal processes that lead to self-organization and self-renewal.

Understanding of constructivist learning theory is essential. Teachers as leaders apply constructivist learning theory to their classroom practices and to the collegial interaction that builds a learning community.

A deep and firsthand understanding of systemic change and transitions is internalized through acceptance that change is full of uncertainty. Teachers as leaders serve their community as facilitators of change, supporting and implementing continual improvements.

An understanding of context is important so that communities build memories, norms, and collegiality. Teachers as leaders celebrate and honor the histories and cultures of their community.

A personal identity that allows for courage and risk, low ego needs, and a sense of possibilities is essential, for teachers as leaders support and facilitate decisions that serve the community as well as individual needs.

These acts and attitudes represent the critical concepts, behaviors, and beliefs that enable teachers as leaders to support, contribute to, and facilitate the development of learning communities.

Moving From Isolation to Collegiality

In her work in coaching schools, one of the first conversations Mary Dietz has with a staff and leadership team addresses relationships among staff members. In one case in which she was coaching an elementary school newly identified as a "restructuring school," it became clear that staff members were just beginning to be congenial with each other. The teachers had a committee to plan breakfast for a staff meeting. It appeared to be the first time they had "broken bread" together. They had worked in isolation for so long that they needed to make conscious efforts to connect, to be congenial. In planning for their first overnight retreat, they brought over 20 videos to fill the evening. They were sure there would be some free time after the evening session, and they were concerned there would be nothing to talk about. They hardly knew each other.

Through a process of asking essential questions, followed by sharing concerns and interests, dialogue emerged. These interests became the focus for practicing dialogue during the day. The retreat offered an opportunity to focus on themselves as part of a community, not as isolated classroom workers. The power of relationships and commitment to community became the force that fueled them toward systemic, lasting changes in their schooling process. They were able to build relationships and to move their conversations from congenial to collegial (Glickman, 1993; Little, 1982). As relationships formed and trust built, community members were able to have collegial conversations. Teachers began taking risks, asking challenging questions about instructional practices and traditional school routines, and reflecting a maturing process as their learning community evolved.

A retreat can be one of the more powerful structures for developing community, yet it can only punctuate frequent, planned and unplanned opportunities for continuous interaction.

Engaging Others in Learning

Moving into collegiality provides multiple opportunities for engaging others in learning processes. As teachers employ leadership actions and embrace leadership attitudes, such involvements build the capacity of the community for learning and, therefore, for leadership. These processes are set within the whole school constructivist learning cycle described above. They involve constructing a shared purpose and collaboration as a means of building learning community. The following are additional examples of actions teachers have taken in their school communities as they seek to form learning communities.

REFLECTIVE ACTION AND CONSTRUCTIVIST COLLABORATIONS

Teachers as leaders invite and honor learning conversations and recognize the importance of reflecting on experiences to continually improve their practice.

Researchers have long told us that teachers make approximately 350 decisions daily; teachers and administrators as well say they sometimes do that in an hour. Teachers are continually reshaping their strategies; listening to students' thinking; reflecting; and redirecting their questioning, content, activities, and expectations. When a school is a learning community, these decisions are more often brought to a conscious level. This begins to happen when teachers collaborate and reflect on decisions they have made, seeking new understandings and feedback. These reflective conversations might take place in a study group, informally during lunch, or at a team planning meeting as they debrief a lesson.

Teachers as leaders incorporate professional development opportunities when they focus on reflective collaborations. Opportunities to collaborate invite teachers to continually expand their repertoires and make conscious, informed decisions that make meaning of their daily experiences and restructure their understandings. They do this by integrating new ideas and reflections of others with their own, a process that requires time and commitment from the school community.

Teachers as leaders seek to build authentic relationships that honor shared memories, encourage risk taking, establish community norms, and develop collegiality. Conversations form the heart of collaboration; conversation engages reflective thought while forming relationships. Lambert et al. (1995) propose that conversations that are constructivist in nature share common elements: shared intention or purpose, search for sense making, remembrance and reflection, revelation of ideas and information, and respectful listening. Such elements describe guiding principles for collaboration and can be discussed (along with others) as a set of preliminary understandings within a community.

What do we mean by "constructivist collaborations"? These are the actions and interactions among willing participants that result in learning. Constructivist collaboration usually involves a combination of talking, listening, observing, doing, thinking, and reflecting. Collaboration has a variety of purposes and is often initiated by a specific focus or need. The process of collaboration may lead to discovering emerging understandings, purposes, and needs. For example, we might listen to understand, to pose questions, to empathize, to focus, or to rethink. We might talk or write to explain or clarify, to interpret, to invent, or to plan. The reciprocal nature of the processes of listening, writing, reflecting, and responding enable new thinking and the restructuring of understandings to occur.

When educators secure collaboration opportunities, they inevitably value and appreciate them. Some examples of conversations that accomplish collaboration goals are the following:

> *Reflective conversations* draw on individuals' repertoire of experiences and understandings as they make connections among prior understandings and new understandings that emerge during the conversation. Often reflective conversations contain responses and interactions that help to clarify, summarize, focus, hypothesize, and invite rethinking.
>
> *Critical friend conversations* involve interactions with colleagues or individuals with whom we have a high level of trust. With these colleagues, we can openly reflect, give and receive feedback, and restructure our thinking. Such supporting conversations are opportunities to openly share emotions and receive acceptance and support. These conversations are usually initiated by sharing reactions and feelings related to an event or topic. Although peer coaching can be among the more powerful forms of critical friend conversations, such collegial coupling can also be less formal and more spontaneous.
>
> *"Round tables" or debriefings* are conversations aimed at communicating, learning, rethinking, hypothesis formation, and developing ideas directly related to an observation or learning activity that has occurred. The Coalition of Essential Schools and the California Center for School Restructuring use a form of reflective debriefing known as the protocol. The *protocol* is a reciprocal team reflective process in which one team listens, poses questions, and makes reflective comments on the work of the other team. In one application of the protocol process, the teams then reverse roles and the presenting team members become reflectors, providing critical friend feedback to their colleagues from the other school.

There are multiple forms of conversations that involve colleagues and other professionals, students, parents, and community members. Most likely, the themes are about teaching and learning.

Below, we propose a few vital factors about teaching and learning that inform the building of learning communities.

The Classroom, Curriculum, and Assessment

Attending to and reframing the teachers' historical role as classroom teacher and developer of curriculum and assessment are vital parts of the process of developing a learning community. Two major reasons underlie this assertion:

1. Teachers as leaders must be respected as good teachers by their colleagues. Unless they have this respect, as we noted in reference to ethics, it is impossible to secure the credibility and authority needed to lead.
2. Teachers as leaders must seek and establish congruence in their professional and personal lives by employing some of the same learning approaches in working with students as they do in working with colleagues.

Teachers as leaders seek strategies and approaches for engaging their students and colleagues. They encourage learners to pose questions of emerging relevance, thereby incorporating their understanding of constructivist learning theory into their classroom practices and community interactions (Brooks & Grennon-Brooks, 1993).

In the classroom, constructivist leadership actions include inviting students to explore and express their current points of view, perceptions, or understandings of a concept. For example, a teacher is in the process of mediating students' understanding of solid geometry. Knowing her students have some familiarity with plane geometric figures such as triangles and squares, she introduces them to solid geometry by having them make polyhedra using origami techniques and materials. She asks them to describe the figure they have just constructed. What are its characteristics? How is the polyhedra similar to and different from the figures they drew on paper earlier in the week? Through their constructions, conversations, and reflections (interactions with people, objects, and ideas), they have restructured their understanding of a geometric figure. They can now expand their understanding of geometry to include solid geometric figures. By monitoring her students' participation, questions, and descriptions, she identifies their current perception of geometric figures as it applies to solid figures. She can then make informed decisions about appropriate next steps for instruction. Imagine applying this constructivist approach with adults. What would it look like?

In addition to constructivist classroom strategies, a central set of assumptions regarding student resiliency (see Chapter 3) challenges teachers to work with the whole child by building sustaining relationships, facilitating social networks among children and with the community, ensuring that the real work of learning involves children in experiences for which they know they are needed, and assisting children to develop a sense of future. These understandings require additional vital role shifts on the part of teachers, including roles as guides, mentors, and long-term facilitators of the lives of children and families. In other words, engaging children as well as adults in learning communities.

Despite the autonomy that teachers often experience in the classroom and in the school, they often feel burdened because of the myriad of items and expectations that are continually added to their "backpacks." They perceive few options for removing existing contents. They would welcome an opportunity to unpack their backpacks and make informed decisions regarding the appropriate and effective items to include. Teachers, working together, are in a prime position to make such decisions regarding the effectiveness of curriculum, assessment, and guidance practices. In their leadership roles, they can join with community members in defining their purpose for schooling and in making curriculum decisions based on those purposes. Such collective decision making would clearly be a shift from a compliant environment in which frameworks are installed, standards imposed, and single measures are used to determine success.

Further, teachers have significant knowledge about when their students and colleagues are learning. They have an obligation to join with countywide, district, state, and federal efforts to refocus and redefine the purpose, meaning, and function of curriculum, assessment, and guidance in the schooling process. Teachers are in a prime position to work with parents and community members regarding these arenas and how they link with learning. They must seize the opportunity to engage parents—in some of the same ways they would engage colleagues—with their child's learning and progress as they learn together about the changes in educational practices. Building sustained relationships with parents as every member of the community works together to learn about innovative practices can ward off extreme reactions to school innovation. Teachers who are constructivist leaders need to take the responsibility to initiate, support, and sustain such a learning community for all members of the community.

Caring About Each Other

A deep sense of ethics requires that we create communities that are caring as well as learning (not that we can separate the two). Who we are and what we do are reciprocal and interdependent. Teachers as leaders need to support policies, practices, and collaborations that help community members feel fulfilled in their work and valued as individuals. Moving from isolation to collegiality requires that the new conditions be supportive and nurturing.

Judy Krupp, a former staff developer devoted to understanding the adult learner, sought to understand the basic human needs of individuals. In her extensive travels, she asked people what it was they wanted most in life. Over a period of 15 years of travel and inquiry, she and her husband identified six basic needs:

- *Good health*, which all individuals seemed to value and understand as a necessity for living and enjoying life
- *Relationships* in which caring and the ability to confide were predominant
- *A positive sense of self*, liking yourself, who you are, and what you stand for
- *Success*, defined differently by the individuals, closely followed by
- *Resourcefulness and flexibility*, being able to adapt to and deal with adversity that may come one's way in life
- *Independence*, the ability to sustain oneself in an independent way for as long as possible in one's lifetime

These six basic needs speak to the heart of the energy source of an individual (Krupp, 1995). What is important to individuals, what their purpose is, and how they connect and contribute to these needs through their work must be considered as we engage the whole person in learning communities. These needs enable us to understand the ecological nature of work and life and the meanings of motivation, willingness, and commitment. These needs inform the importance of structures that enable us to care and learn together.

Creating Structures That Build Learning Communities

Teachers as leaders are continually questioning and refining the structures, processes, and approaches they employ in building and sustaining community learning. These undertakings necessitate a few guidelines.

Advocate for learning time. Imagine teaching in a school where the norm is for teachers and administrators to meet on a regular basis to debrief lessons, examine student work, and make adaptations; to pose questions about schoolwide issues and initiate an inquiry process; and to hold round tables regarding student, educator, and school assessment. Teachers as leaders need to advance a plan for professional time. Some strategies for finding professional time suggested by Gary Watts and Shari Castle in their article, "The Time Dilemmas in School Restructuring," were (a) freed-up time (e.g., inviting administrators, assistants, college interns, or parents to cover classes); (b) restructured or rescheduled time (e.g., altering the school schedule to provide a late arrival or early dismissal for students one day a week or working in teams where pairs can plan while peers are with students); (c) common time (e.g., scheduling common planning time for colleagues with similar assignments); (d) better-used time (e.g., using faculty meetings for staff development); and (e) purchased time (e.g., using staff development funds to pay for half- or full-day miniretreats for teachers) (Watts & Castle, 1993). An extended year will become increasingly essential as we join together to resolve the complex problems of schooling. Time takes on even greater significance when we expand the notion of professional time to learning time that involves students as well as adults. Although the structuring of time alone will not reform our schools, it will go a long way toward reform if we apply two major criteria for the new uses of time. First, extended time (e.g., block scheduling) must allow for *depth and authentic work,* including service to others. Second, extended time (e.g., multigrade, multiyear groupings) must allow for *sustained relationships* by working with the same teacher and children for two or more years. When time is restructured with an eye to the purposes of increased and different interaction patterns—therefore different relationships—it becomes a major factor in the reform of schooling.

Develop structures focused on a given purpose or issue; have clear expectations and roles; give substantive attention to dialogue, reflection, and inquiry; and have an expectation that the structure will change when the work is done. These criteria can create "nested" learning communities that usually emerge from the self-organizing tendencies of a learning community. It is vital that the restructured system provide for personal feedback loops with the rest of the community and for the circulation of information from beyond the school. Personal feedback loops mean in-person, not just written communications with colleagues as the work proceeds. The connections beyond the school might include access to an additional research community or literature, inclusion of district office personnel, connection with a professional network, involvement of university faculty in study groups (see "Professional Development Schools," pp. 91-92 in this text).

Develop governance structures that are sustainable. Shared decision making and site based management have been two popular school reform strategies during this decade. The purpose and meaning of shared decision making have been frequently misunderstood, largely because school communities have not identified the purpose and context for decision making as well as the process and procedures for making decisions. Involving the community in decision making is vital to the development of learning communities, so it is important to consider many approaches and groupings. Many schools find leadership teams effective, using the same guidelines for formation that we described in Number 2 above. It is essential that such groups have overlapping membership in order to sustain continuity over time.

Reframe the use of whole-group meetings. Small-group time is essential, but it is not a substitute for the whole faculty getting together to talk, inquire, and construct meanings. Such a goal requires that we recast faculty meetings as professional development time, as well as using large-group strategies on staff development days and in retreats. The dynamics of the whole are essential in the creation of a positive school culture and learning community; otherwise, over time, the relationships and work become fragmented.

If a staff is small, working as a whole group is not a problem. However, if the staff is in a large high school, it is more difficult. There are numerous effective strategies now for working with large groups. For more detailed information about large-group strategies, we would refer readers to the work of Suzanne Bailey with the Bailey Alliance in Vacaville, California (see Bailey, 1995a).

Involve diverse voices in each structure. Governing bodies, study groups, and all community structures benefit from diverse membership and perspectives. When forming such groups, ask, Who should be at the table? Then ask, Who have we left out? Often students, new teachers, parents, district personnel, community members, cooperating agency personnel, and university faculty are not considered. Take into consideration such issues as influence and power, who will be affected by the work, and who can bring special or unique perspectives or expertise. Ultimately, remember that connection and relationship between diverse elements in the community is one of the most important strategies of ecosystems and of life in general. In dense, complex, well-connected networks, divisions among people and groups are less likely to occur.

Seek to enhance the professionalism of professional organizations. Teachers as leaders have an opportunity to influence the perceptions and expectations of professional teachers' organizations by ensuring that union conversations aim at teachers as professionals. They must join together to move away from being controlled by patriarchal practices in a system built on compliance and strive to form a professional community with mature relationships and shared responsibilities. In many states, teachers' unions are primary structures that direct the professional activities of teachers and their professional standing in the school community. Teachers' unions could encourage and build capacity for teacher leadership by the guidelines, expectations, and negotiated items they advocate for in their relationship with the school community at large.

Design accountability structures that work. It is essential that educators collaboratively design accountability structures that enable them to know if their plans are being carried out and working. In

Chapter 6, we will discuss further the importance of holding each other accountable for the quality of the learning environment. However, the learning cycle embedded in the reflection and inquiry that we propose is, in itself, an accountability structure; for it is the evidence that emerges from these processes that helps us to understand our accomplishments. In addition, relationships, such as coaching, can enable educators to focus on the common purpose of the school as participants ask each other critical questions about what they intend: Is it meeting their expectations? What is the evidence? How do they make sense of what they are seeing? What are the implications for action? In Chapter 8, we will connect alternative teacher evaluation to these forms of accountability.

These guidelines can be helpful in developing structures that will deepen and widen the learning and leading relationships in a school. They serve as the place in which learning, leading, and collegiality occur and grow. These principles for developing structures can bring coherence to what sometimes feels like a fragmented professional life. The development of a learning community will bring commitment to change and growth as well, for learning is at the root of building commitment to change (Fullan, 1994).

Examples of Structures and Organizers for Building Learning Communities in Schools

The New York City chapter of the United Federation of Teachers recently published a document titled, "Teacher for the 21st Century." The purpose of this publication is to address the principles of professional teaching. They reflect guidelines for professional practice and contribute to moving the teaching profession into the domain of accepting responsibility for professional practice. In designing an implementation process for these principles, they considered structures and organizers that might contribute to teachers' ongoing development within the school system. This led to offering alternative teacher evaluation processes. They invited tenured teachers to consider alternative evaluation structures that focused on learning and building collegial relationships, such as participation in study groups, action research projects, professional development portfolios, and peer coaching. In the spirit of teachers as learners and leaders, we think it is important to consider structures, organizers, and processes that contribute to building learning communities in schools. The following examples engage the work and examples of our coauthors as they share their experiences with professional development portfolios, action research, study groups, networks as learning communities, and professional development schools. These examples represent powerful approaches toward the development of learning communities—strategies that are actually in use.

The Professional Development Portfolio

The professional development portfolio is a structure and process that supports learning and contributes to establishing new norms for the ongoing professional development of educators. Using the portfolio as a collection of items, such as a *presentation portfolio* for exhibiting and/or recording professional accomplishments for teachers, was first documented by Kenneth Wolf in 1991. His article reflects the Teacher Assessment Project (TAP) at Stanford with Lee Shulman. This project was to assist with the ultimate design and plans for the National Board of Teaching Standards, which introduced the notion of *working portfolio*, a process in which the nature of the artifacts and evidences collected and exhibited by the learner are directed by others.

In 1987, Mary Dietz refined the design and process of the professional development portfolio while working with Mariam True at the Professional Development Consortium in San Diego, California. In the consortium's pilot project, teachers used *learner portfolios*, a portfolio structure and process that was teacher directed and supported by the school system and peer collaboration.

As it was first used, the professional development portfolio was a framework or organizer to focus and facilitate reflection and collaboration regarding professional practices. The focus for learning, or essential question, was learner-generated and aimed at connecting the needs and interests of individuals with their work and with the purpose of schooling in their school community. The professional development portfolio was designed around four organizers (Dietz, 1993):

- *Purpose*—Why are you doing a professional development portfolio?

- *Focus*—What will be your entry point or theme for learning?
- *Process*—How and with whom will you collaborate, learn, and reflect?
- *Outcomes*—What have you learned and what do you want to do next?

The caution is that most portfolios are used as a collection of "things" to be viewed, and in some cases evaluated, by another without the learner being present. The process we are talking about goes beyond that. It is an organizer or framework for deepening the levels of understanding, exploration, and assimilation of new thinking into one's practice. It is not done in isolation, it is not measured by a rubric, and it is not directed by a consumable goal. Portfolios that have gone in that single dimension have lost the dynamic of inquiry, collaboration, and reflection for learning. This is significant when we consider our mission of teachers becoming self-directed and asserting leadership actions. The portfolio is a structure that allows for role flexibility, dialogue, and conversation. It is reciprocal, not hierarchical, and it invites uncertainty as well as the continual structuring and restructuring of thinking.

Many school districts have made the commitment to build learning communities for teachers. Some have used a combination of portfolio types as they design a process that reflects the purposes of their portfolio. An example of a derivation of the portfolio process is the *school portfolio*, a portfolio that represents the work, focus or entry point, and outcomes of schoolwide change efforts. The process of selecting, collecting, and reflecting on artifacts and evidences that represent the evolving process of the school system and the purpose of schooling contributes to the emergence of the school's "voice." Reflections that accompany the collection tell the story of the school as a community: its purpose and its journey.

Many positive results have occurred as a result of offering these learning opportunities to teachers. Dr. Sharing Graves at the University of Ohio, Dayton, conducted a four-year case study that revealed the following benefits from the portfolio process (Graves, 1995):

- Teachers found the professional development portfolio to be an excellent framework to gain focus on their personal and professional growth.

- Portfolio development stages were different for each participant.
- Teachers needed time to adjust to having control over their own professional growth.
- After having engaged in the process, teachers no longer felt the need to follow the organization; they had internalized the process.
- Learning to self-assess took time, feedback, and rethinking on the part of teachers.

These benefits represent an important reason for teachers to take charge of their own professional development and learning.

Action Research

Another example of a structure and process for building learning communities is *action research*—inquiry into practice within the context that we work, either classroom, whole school, district, or community. Although various forms of action research have been part of the work of teaching since Dewey wrote about reflection and action decades ago, the recent revival of action research as integrated into the work of teaching provides a setting for establishing learning communities among teachers and their administrator colleagues. The research enterprise brings teachers (including those who are working as administrators) together in defining a focus and purpose for their inquiry. A community is formed as school-based researchers collaborate to plan their work, collect and analyze their data, and so forth. Like its corollary in the university research community, action research involves a systematic inquiry designed to illuminate an issue, question, problem, or dilemma puzzling the researchers. Questions of practice guide the work of teacher research: for example, how particular children learn mathematics, what strategies produce better reading outcomes among particular children, how teachers collaborate effectively to bring about change, and what forms of resistance inhibit school reform—all these are topics familiar to the teacher research community.

Similar to the informal interrogation of practice conducted by thoughtful teachers on a daily basis, action research is designed to improve the work of schooling. Teachers, administrators, and other adults who are part of the school community can come together as a community of learners to examine their work in systematic ways and to draw from this examination a plan for subsequent action. This direct connection between inquiry and action is one factor that distinguishes teacher research from other research in education. In traditional, university-based research, the connection to action is frequently much less direct and is usually outside of the purview of the researchers themselves.

As a mechanism for examining various aspects of school life in a careful and systematic manner, action research is a powerful learning opportunity for participants. They talk together, work together, solve problems together, and learn together. The actual work of these collaborative conversations takes a variety of forms within the research process. Sometimes teachers examine various aspects of the same problem and contribute their data and analysis to the larger goal. At other times, teachers work together on the same problem, analyzing the same evidence, capitalizing on the different lenses the different researchers bring. Because of the learning community created when action researchers work together, the process is also an important locus for school reform.

Communities of teacher researchers are common now in many parts of the United States. The Bay Area Writing Project, now expanded to be a National Writing Project, involves large numbers of teachers conducting research and writing about their teaching and their schoolwork. Because of their collaborative efforts, which have resulted in teachers learning about the work of schooling together, the effects of the writing project are seen in many school reform programs. Practice changes when teachers define problems, examine them together in systematic ways, and take those findings back to the school communities where they work.

In California, the Bay Region IV Professional Development Consortium conducts an extensive teacher research program that focuses on school reform itself. The researchers in this project, which has now expanded to include teachers as well as school administrators, work together in teams of two or more to investigate and inform the school change process at their particular sites. In addition to the teaming of teachers by school, the researchers form a network that connects their work with that of other research teams from seven Bay Area counties. The network gathers for several full-day collaborative research meetings each year in which the researchers discuss their process and findings and learn about research methodologies that guide them in their work. Interestingly, whether the project focuses on the school as a whole, as does the Bay Region IV Project, or the classroom in particular, practice is affected and the school reform effort advanced. One teacher in the Bay Region network reflected on her research study and its impact:

> If you look at what does work and what doesn't on the whole school level, I have to transfer that into my classroom. It's really caused me to analyze why I do some things that I do. Some things I do because somebody told me that it was a good thing to do. And maybe it is, but now I know why. It's made me more analytical of what I do in the classroom and what I want for my students. . . . It's an exercise that's made an impact on how I teach. (Stacey, in Richert, 1994, p. 6)

Research on the Bay Region IV Action Research Project revealed that the network process resulted in the researchers feeling more confident about their work in schools, more knowledgeable about school change, more likely to assume leadership roles, better able to communicate with colleagues, and more knowledgeable about the role of learning in teaching than they were before they were researchers (Richert, 1994).

There are many features of action research as a process that underscore the role of learning in teaching and leading and the power of a learning community for directing the course of change in schools. In the action research process, teachers examine questions that are important to them. As they draw from their experience questions that matter to them most, they become more aware of themselves as definers and constructors of knowledge and more aware of the power of their ideas. Similarly, as they share their questions with colleagues and work with those colleagues to search for answers, those who know most about particular questions provide leadership in formulating the questions and designing the inquiry. Teams of teachers and administrators are able to work together to do research. The process

itself is more powerful when done in collaboration, as the participants contribute their knowledge, expertise, insight, and energy to
the various stages of the process. Furthermore, because the process
generates documentation that can be shared with the profession
more broadly, a larger network is formed, and the professional community is enhanced. Teacher research is thus one means by which
participants in an educational community can come together to construct and direct school change. As one teacher researcher in the Bay
Region IV Project explained,

> I've come to a conclusion due to my research activity these
> past several years: Doing the research—the interviews, the
> reading, the reflection, that is, the process of research—is, or
> should be, a major goal for all restructuring schools. (Dan, as
> cited in Richert, 1994, p. 9)

The Learning Community Model: Graduate Education

At Hamline University in St. Paul, Minnesota, experienced
teachers enrolled in graduate education programs are creating professional learning communities. The master's degree program at
Hamline University is a young program, created to respond to midcareer teachers who seek advanced study. The child of two parents,
Liberal Studies and Professional Development, the program seeks to
balance liberal study and interdisciplinary thought with appropriate
evaluation and attention to inquiry. The learning communities are
hosted in school districts that are members of a local, nonprofit consortium of public schools. The consortium has partnered with leaders
at the university to improve the effectiveness of graduate education
for teachers.

These learning communities are groups of experienced teachers
that collaborate with facilitators to study issues of importance to their
work. Teachers and facilitators share ideas, create relationships, and
build trust among themselves and with their new colleagues. The
framework of the "curriculum" is drawn from several philosophi-
cally compatible strands that create a learning model respectful of
adult learning and built on comprehensive assessment. This model

of learning has been called progressive (Dewey), constructivist (Brooks & Grennon-Brooks, 1993), open education (Barth, 1988), and emanicipatory (Freìre, 1970). Three strands that were consistently addressed through teachers' reflections were struggles to embrace a type of graduate education that was emanicipatory, the importance of collegial support, and the integration of personal and professional development.

Each learning community is made up of 45 to 50 teachers guided by two or three facilitators who are teacher educators. Collectively, the full communities identify professional issues; reframe the core course requirements to fit the group's goals; and identify ways individuals, small groups of teachers, and the whole group can meet the criteria for program completion. The small groups function in a variety of ways.

First, each advisory, or collegial group, constructs itself. The advisory groups are not formed until the full community has had time to group and regroup in several subcommittees: site-based groups, interest-alike groups, grade-alike groups, and random groups. After people are well acquainted with their own strengths and interests as well as those of their colleagues, they create advisory groups that remain intact for the life of the learning community.

Second, these groups are authentic. They are charged with interpreting the assessment framework for the criteria of the program's curriculum core requirements and creating criteria for the small group members and for individuals within it. They are also responsible for articulating criteria for the broader program outcomes, such as those represented by the National Board for Professional Standards.

Third, these groups create a safety zone for trust building, skill development, and leading that may be less accessible in the large group of 50 or in one's school setting. Within these safety zones, new colleagues with a shared agenda find support, encouragement, acknowledgment, and opportunities to take risks. One of the risks teachers took was that of leading within their small groups.

In addition, advisory groups served as a place for the articulation of one's beliefs as an educator. As ideas and actions arose from the large group, these subgroups of self-organized, nested learning communities provided the catalyst for the individual meaning making necessary for the translation of ideas and actions into practice.

Collegial support became the strongest component of the communities. One participant commented,

> What I need in an advisory group is support. I need to be able to give and receive curriculum ideas. I need constructive criticism and guidance when things are not working out. I need to be able to talk frankly about my feelings, personal or work related, and feel that I am safe and that people are listening. . . . I need to be validated as an educator as well as be able to validate the others in my group for what they are doing.

These advisory groups became reciprocal caring communities, as noted by a second participant:

> Not only has my advisory group been supportive of my role as an educator, but they have also been understanding and caring enough to listen to personal concerns that have developed during the past year due to my role as student and learner. They have affirmed me as a person and as a valuable member of the group.

Another important aspect of the nested groups was the emergence of leadership behaviors. Young teachers with little experience in formal leadership roles in schools had opportunities to meet with colleague groups, form their own ideas, and present them for consideration.

Three forms of assessment were used in the groups. Each advisory group worked to devise an evaluation framework against which they would present their professional portfolios at the conclusion of the program. Using the five propositions of the National Board for Professional Teaching Standards as a framework, each learning community developed a set of criteria that would be used by its membership. This process served as a crossroads or meeting point in the real life of these teachers, their specific curriculum needs, and the externally created board standards. In addition, each member of the group conducted an applied research project. As the program drew to a close, the advisory groups met with their facilitator teams to present their portfolios. Within that presentation, members spoke often about the support and safety the advisory group created so that each could venture into this new, uncharted territory (Collay & Gagnon, 1995).

Professional Development Schools

During most of this century, many universities had "lab schools" attached to their campuses or situated nearby. The purpose of the laboratory school was to prepare student teachers and to conduct research, although often in a setting that did not represent the actual world of schooling. Lab schools were typically attended by the children of university faculty and other children living near the university. The schools often felt like "hothouses," protected environments in which the real and challenging problems of schooling were minimized.

By the late 1970s, many of these lab schools had ceased to exist. However, the need for a focused setting in which to prepare educators continued, and by the mid-1980s, the issuance of the Holmes Report (Holmes Group, Inc., 1990) brought forth a new concept in laboratory schools. This new conception, known as the *professional development school*, is a real, thriving school, not an artificially constructed one. These schools are often in the center of urban areas, rich with the diversity of family and neighborhood issues confronting most urban schools today.

These schools and the universities choose each other, entering into a dynamic and reciprocal partnership that is designed to improve both the school and the university. They are schools in the process of getting better, schools in which staff are self-reflective and struggling to find approaches to work with some of the most challenging urban issues of our time. There are hundreds of professional development schools in the United States today that are a part of an international network.

Describing the promise of professional development schools, Linda Darling-Hammond (1996) points out that "a growing number of education schools are working with school systems to create Professional Development Schools that will prepare teachers for what schools must *become,* not only schools as they *are*" (p. 6). This process of becoming is a central feature of the professional development school, particularly in reference to the emergence of teacher leadership.

The collaborative nature of the school-university partnership involves the teaming of university professors with school teachers and is diffusing the hypercritical focus on the solitary teacher leader. The mere sustained presence of university educators creates a consciousness about the importance of the work at hand and focuses attention on the central purpose of the common work. The professional development school has enabled a new form of collegial leadership to emerge among the teachers. This common work can be successful in focusing on a shared purpose, collaboration, and building community.

It is important to note that all of these efforts are not successful merely by design. In many cases, professional development schools have turned out to be just another teacher placement rather than a setting for doing joint work for whole school change (the "becoming" dimension of which Darling-Hammond spoke). At California State University, Hayward, Linda Lambert and her colleagues are discovering that it is important to involve departments of educational leadership and administration, as well as teacher education. In this way, understandings about school culture, leadership, and systemic change are more likely to be part of the perspective that university faculty bring to the partnership.

Conclusion

These structures and organizers invite and facilitate the following development opportunities for professional teachers:

- Authentic learning and leading—one conversation at a time
- Deep levels of conversation and reflection—regarding their work
- Focused inquiry and exploration of professional practices
- Continual rethinking of the purpose and function of schooling

All of these opportunities contribute to developing attitudes, experiences, and understandings for building and supporting learning communities in schools. They require commitment of time and other resources and a belief that we cannot control others, make them change, or impose new ideas. For individuals to learn, develop, and assume leadership roles, they must be involved in a community of learning.

We believe teachers can save our schools. They are the professional practitioners who work with students every day—nourishing their minds, supporting their resilience, offering them academic rigor, and modeling respect. They are the ones who do the primary work in teaching and learning and who understand the purpose and meaning of their work from firsthand experience. The vantage point of the classroom teacher is critical in understanding the schooling system and its strengths and weaknesses. Teachers lead through facilitating learning communities.

Teaching as Leading

IN MANY PARTS OF THE UNITED STATES, THE teacher's voice is beginning to be heard in conversations about restructuring schools. Although teachers, because they work directly with children, may have the greatest effect on the success of the school, they are seldom called on to lead the process of school reform. Therefore, many teachers do not see themselves as leaders of adults or of the profession. Furthermore, the more visible teacher leaders are continually encouraged to leave the classroom and work directly with adult colleagues.

Our assumptions about the need for formal leadership and authority in schools are implicit in current educational practice: Teachers work with children, and designated leaders work with adults; teachers are isolated, have little time set aside to prepare their lessons and complete administrative tasks, and have virtually no time designated for adult interaction. A newly certified teacher is expected to shoulder the same responsibilities as a 30-year veteran, revealing our tacit belief that experienced teachers do nothing differently than newcomers. Teachers who survive this enculturation and still surface as able adults are seen as "true leaders" and urged to become administrators. This tradition of school leadership predates this century with little change in recent years.

The lack of professional status for those who remain in teaching is reflected in current tensions that face teachers who choose to stay in classrooms. Can they really provide leadership from the teacher's role? Or does the gendered nature of teaching or the child-centered focus of the work limit potential to lead? Our conversation about the constructivist leader opens doors to new possibilities for career teachers to be school leaders and for formal leaders to remain engaged in the activities of teaching and learning that initially drew them to the profession. We believe that good teaching is itself constructivist leadership and that teachers are key participants in facilitating the construction of knowledge in schools. This chapter focuses on the teacher's leadership role as meaning maker with children and as meaning maker in school-level leadership. This foundation must be firmly anchored before teachers will open their doors to their roles as reformers.

In Chapter 1, we identified the dominance of the female gender in teaching as a major context issue. To further make sense of the emergent roles of teacher leaders, we must understand the journey teachers have taken to become professionals. The role of teacher is closely linked with children, and the nurturance of children has not often been framed as leadership. Historically, leadership theories and beliefs have been steeped in the metaphors of the "great men" role models (see Chapter 2) studied in social studies textbooks, in graduate education in leadership and organizational theory, and in contemporary business "how-to" books. As women have taken more formal roles in leadership, they have been influenced by these traditions of leadership. Until recently, women in formal leadership have accepted the same Western, Newtonian approaches to leadership as men. In the late 20th century, however, theories of leadership have begun to evolve as a growing understanding of, and respect for, more holistic and integrated leadership approaches have emerged. Teachers, traditionally perceived as followers, are contributing to a more organic model of organizational reform and change.

Because schools have been female dominant and male led, women and men teachers have accepted roles as followers of primarily male principals. This condition may contribute heavily to the failure to place responsibility for school reform in the hands of teachers. Whereas some regions report a growing number of women in formal leadership roles, the national picture shows only modest changes (Bell & Chase, 1993; Schmuck & Shubert, 1995). The gendered difference between leader (male) and follower (female) widens the chasm of power and authority and replicates industrial divisions between management and staff. Although many teachers now seek advanced degrees while remaining in the classroom, thereby bringing a greater foundation of knowledge and expertise to the role of teacher, mainstream cultural beliefs about appropriate roles of women and men continue to limit understanding of teaching as a profession. These limitations hinge partly on beliefs about whether women can even be professionals (Preston, 1991). Despite these deeply ingrained practices, change in educational roles is occurring.

Evidence of change in both assumptions about the role of teacher and organizational practices in schools can be seen in the number of experienced teachers who attain advanced degrees and remain in the classroom. Since the early 1960s, the percentage of teachers holding a master's degree or six-year diploma has more than doubled (Darling-Hammond, 1990). The knowledge base attained in graduate study can move a teacher from one who is subjected to orders to one who is a decision maker, from factory hand to one who is responsible for a greater societal good. Title and role, such as principal and teacher, still separate management from staff; but in recent years, teachers have sought opportunities to extend their capacity in the classroom and are usually as knowledgeable, if not more so, than their principals. This professional transition has provided more opportunities for teachers to be seen as leaders. More important, diverging roles encourage teachers to see themselves as leaders.

A second important change is the slow but steady efforts of teachers to establish collegial relationships within their schools. As we noted in Chapters 1 and 3, the nature of the industrial model school limits collegial interaction between adults. Teachers who value opportunities to enhance their professional status struggle to overcome the organizational structures that limit this development. Experienced teachers are dependent on strong collegial relationships for their continued development (Kent, 1985, as cited in Little, 1990).

A third important change that supports the contributions of teachers to new images of leadership is the epistemological movement toward constructivist teaching and learning in schools. As teachers gain courage to collaborate in the construction of new learning with their students, they can envision collaborating with colleagues in the same way. As we have noted, collegial interaction is possible only in a culture of mutual respect and care for the other. It is not feasible in authoritarian or hierarchical structures. As we reimagine learning in constructivist ways, we know more about how to construct knowledge with children than with adults. Although one experience doesn't necessarily precede the other, the sheer number of hours teachers spend with children provides many more opportunities for learning about constructing learning with children than with adults.

These changes give us faith that teachers, in the current context of educational reform, are uniquely poised to effect real change in schools. Although they have always been so poised, the changes in our thinking about systems and reform described in this book are creating real opportunities and support for teachers to see themselves as change agents. Teachers have called the question and are seeking answers. It must be teachers themselves, however, who begin to present their work with children as leadership. One hundred years of tradition will not slip quietly away.

Are teaching and leading the same? We know that in effective classrooms, adults and children construct knowledge together, develop shared meanings, and are participants in creating a learning community. Adults provide these opportunities for construction of new knowledge because they are leading children along a pathway to knowledge. Adults who lead other adults hope for the same capacity building and growth in knowledge for the members of their organizations. There are lessons from teaching that can inform our understanding of learning and leadership.

How Are Teachers Currently Leading?

Teachers talk about children. They talk about individual children, about how different children learn, and about what strategies might lead those individual children into new understandings of their world. Teachers talk about their roles as facilitators of the learning of others, as stewards of communities of learners. They seldom discuss budgets, policies, or turf—topics that are more common at administrative meetings. If we look beyond the client and the context, however, we may see some interesting parallels in the construction of knowledge, or meaning making, by teachers and administrators. The beliefs they share may be the keys that unlock successful school restructuring.

We believe that good teachers are constructivist leaders. In her discussion about the role of teachers in school restructuring, Rallis (1989) describes the leader as a "catalyst, guide, interpreter, and facilitator for a process" (p. 201). Many teachers, especially those who work with younger students, embrace those terms. The practicing teacher is herself a constructivist leader in the school, modeling learning for students and sharing learning with other adults in the school community. A parallel practice may emerge between leadership with adults and leadership with children as the role of teacher-leader, one who creates an environment in which participants are encouraged to make their own meaning from their own experiences. Many teachers cite the importance of building of relationships with children, "in order to reach them." This time-worn adage holds much truth, because new learning does not occur in a linear, decontextualized setting. Learning is reciprocal, as both "teacher" and "learner" become teacher and learner (Freìre, 1970). The reciprocal processes delineated in Chapter 2 provide a common language for us to examine the reflections of practicing teachers as they portray their understanding of their work.

The research that informs this conversation comes from two sources: a study of first-year teachers describing how they are learning to teach and a study of experienced teachers who have recently completed a Master of Arts in Education and have chosen to stay in the classroom. These first excerpts of teacher talk are taken from interview transcripts in a yearlong ethnographic study of new teachers. New teachers talked about their roles within teaching as counselor, empowerer, and learner. We see the early stages of "catalyst and guide" in the words of teachers articulating beliefs and making meaning of their role as teacher. These young teachers are engaging with individual students to construct learning opportunities. Their reflections about the children's learning and their own learning are completely intertwined.

Teachers Describe Their Role

The teachers in this first section were participants in a study of five new teachers who were enrolled in a resident-year master's degree program. They had already obtained a license, were completely responsible for a classroom, and looked much like any other first-year teacher. They met on a weekly basis for seminar and with their supervisor each week in their classroom. The text that follows came from individual interviews conducted throughout their first year of teaching. Susan, Thad, Marilyn, and Terry taught in small, rural districts, whereas Barbara was in a suburban, blue-collar area. The geographic setting was the northwestern United States.

Susan taught English 7 and 8 and Home Economics in a tiny rural high school of about 200 students grades 7 through 12. She described the dilemma of a senior named Annie, who had recently chosen to walk with a different friend in the graduation ceremony and had alienated her peers:

> So Annie's hurting from that. She says the whole class hates her. Annie's feeling victimized right now. And I'm hearing from other people that she brought it on herself, and so I want to say, "It's going to be OK." I try to get in my counselor mode.

Susan paid close attention to the emotional state of this young woman, and her focus in this remark was to nurture and support this student through a difficult time. She saw her role as counselor and named it as such.

Another new teacher, Marilyn, reflects on a 7-year-old in her charge:

> I think I've brought Hanna out of her very quiet shell. You know what I've been doing, I've been giving her lots of hugs.

Again, the focus is on the role of teacher as counselor, one who nurtures and supports children in their quests to become themselves. The focus for these teachers is the child's environment, an awareness that a high level of anxiety will diminish opportunity for learning. An important role for the teacher is creating a trusting environment for learning.

In this next conversation, Barbara discusses a young man in her fifth-grade class. She had previously expressed her intent to teach her students to become responsible for themselves:

> If I could get him in a situation where I could push him over that little hump, have him finish something and feel good

about it, maybe he would take that initiative on, become more self-motivated. I think students have to learn to resolve problems themselves, but when I see that they're struggling with that, and they're not getting anywhere, sometimes I will give them tools to resolve their problems.

In these descriptions, new teachers are quite aware of their role as guide or catalyst. The act of teaching begins with identification of these students' emotional needs, as these three teachers articulate in their analyses. After giving a description and an interpretation of the child's behaviors, these teachers made choices about which values to encourage. Those values came from teachers' individual beliefs, from the culture of the school, and from the expectations of the greater society. The literature on constructivist education suggests a need for the development of shared values and beliefs. Within the learning community of the classroom, these teachers begin with individual needs, make choices and decisions that reflect their own values, then lead the students toward a collaboratively constructed, rather than a predetermined outcome. Qualities desired in a leader, such as vision and management skills, are required to create such a constructive environment. Yet the teacher is engaging the other participants, who are children, in the act of constructing knowledge. And because they construct the learning together, the traditionally distinct roles of leader and follower are not useful. Understanding that all individuals are capable of leading and participating provides a more helpful interpretation for constructivist teaching and leading.

Another quality of a teacher who is a constructivist leader is the capacity to share power. Again, metaphors from corporate, masculine cultures are not sufficient for the classroom. A woman caring for children is seen as "providing for." A thoughtful leader values expanded capacity in the other members of the community, especially if they are youngsters. In this next example, Susan demonstrates a strong commitment to empowering the learner. Her classroom activities were structured to create an environment in which young adolescents would become more individual in their thinking:

My seventh graders are so self-confident right now that they don't feel like they always have to group together and always believe the same way to be liked by each other.

In this excerpt, Susan assumes she has framed actions that will embody new behaviors, in her and in her students. Her students are able to build community with each other in a more healthy, interdependent way.

Any teacher or parent of adolescents has bemoaned the "peer problem" as their children become teenagers and look to each other, rather than to adults, for guidance. Each of us has struggled with the right form of leadership for this age group, a form that is recognized both by the young people and by the adult community as appropriate for a time of transition. The qualities of a "guide" are especially useful, because adult role modeling can be the most powerful balance for students.

For Thad, with a fifth-sixth split class of young adolescents, the notion of "guide" proved elusive. In one conversation, he described appropriate classroom atmosphere as "definitely no spitwads, no throwing things . . . if an assignment comes up, the kids will greet it with, if not with enthusiasm, at least with acceptance." A positive ambiance would be "just a feeling of peace, that the kids are working it out, or just playing a game, or just talking between them, really getting along." In response to a question about his role in creating such an atmosphere, he replied, "I have a major role. Because, I don't see the kids creating it for themselves." Whereas his classroom teaching proved a fairly negative and unsuccessful experience, he described having greater success as a scout leader "taking kids into the wilderness, where they have to listen up the first time. I say something and that's it." Exerting authority felt comfortable to Thad in the outdoor setting where the cues about what the children needed were evident to him. Thad described a hike he took with the fifth graders at the end of a very tough year:

> So I bought treats—chips, juice, and apples—and we went hiking up the creek a ways. And I said, "OK, what have we learned from times we have gone out in the woods before? Keep in a line, keep together, have a person at the head of the line and the tail, and just be really organized."

Inside the classroom, Thad was insecure about his role as "authority," whereas outside, traditional leadership seemed a comfortable fit. In this case, "guide" was not collaborative but authoritative.

In the next excerpt, we are reminded that younger children need a leader who values them and believes in their ability to accomplish tasks. Marilyn and Barbara had a similar empowerment agenda for their students. Marilyn reflected at the end of her first year:

> If I teach second grade again, I'd let them do more of the actual teaching, have them do more of the investigating and the reporting, even from the beginning . . . just let them take more responsibility.

This teacher faced a personal dilemma of returning the responsibility of constructing new knowledge to the children. She was a teacher who initially tried to package every piece of learning in small, bite-sized pieces, and only through trial and error did she begin to relinquish that grip.

This shift could also be portrayed as a "break set" behavior on Marilyn's part. New teachers carry the image of "teacher up front" from their years as students and are therefore socialized to provide answers to questions. Her choice to give "more responsibility" is a choice to share the construction of new knowledge, not to hand it over prepackaged. This is also a choice to be a different kind of teacher, or leader. The confidence to make this shift in perspective comes from different sources, we believe. Daily life in the classroom is itself a disrupter of the stereotype of teacher, as experienced teachers see results from collaborative instruction that they will not see from direct instruction. Alert teachers soon realize that instruction delivered from the front doesn't take. The repertoire of teaching strategies expands as new teachers become more willing and able to change the ways they structure learning. Confidence in one's emerging role as a collaborator is also essential, as children and adolescents respond positively to invitations to share the creation of the environment for learning.

Finally, acceptance by senior colleagues is critical for new teachers. Until they feel some sense of membership in the association of teachers, they may not be willing to try out new behaviors. Even so, a teacher who builds capacity in others rather than behaving in the more traditional role of teacher as teller is often criticized by colleagues who retain a different view of the role of teacher and may find himself or herself "teaching against the grain" (Cochran-Smith,

1991). If teachers feel criticism while "teaching like leaders," what implications are there for those who see themselves as leaders teachers? Barbara summed up her beliefs this way:

> I like to find more seeds to plant and find ways of pulling out that kind of learning rather than just give them a book and have them read questions and write answers.

Barbara is not only a guide but a facilitator of the learning of others. For the learner to construct knowledge, each must be nurtured by other learners in a safe environment. Barbara concluded:

> The more responsibility that I can get students to take on, the better I feel, because I feel they're more prepared to deal with the outside world.

A key to constructivist leadership by teachers is the belief that they must facilitate the conditions for learning, not do the work of learning for their students. In a culture in which teaching is telling, teachers are sometimes considered lacking the ability to discipline if they are found supporting active learners. A colleague may wonder aloud from the doorway, "Who's in charge here?" As any teacher leader can tell us, facilitating the learning of others is much harder than telling. Facilitation is also much more effective and satisfying if the goal of the teacher and leader is to build strength in others. In a community of learners, adults must be trusted to support the learning of children without threat of criticism by colleagues and administrators. The presence of a true community of learners is necessary for this trust building.

Constructing knowledge is a multifaceted process for the classroom teacher, and the context of the learning of others frames individual teacher development as well. As we have discussed in our chapter on learning communities, one must acknowledge one's own growth as a learner and the effects of others on our learning. This understanding requires reflection on one's own learning and behaviors as a leader or collaborator with others, as well as reflection on the learning of others. Some may assume that only experienced teachers have the maturity to reflect on their own learning, yet these beginners reflected copiously while still on the earliest leg of their professional journeys. Statements of self-examination and reflection were found throughout interviews with these new teachers. In this interview, Terry wondered how she could possibly get through the third-grade curriculum before the end of the year:

> And I thought, "All right, I gotta do this. I gotta do this, I gotta do this, I can't do it all in one day, I can't do it all in one year!" Yeah. I've lightened up! I decided, "What are my priorities?" And I decided my priorities are that they learn how to read, and learn how to write, and actually write with some sort of idea of being able to proof and see what their writing's about.

These first attempts at self-dialogue reflect early efforts to reconstruct old assumptions in a school culture not given to breaking set with myths. In Terry's case, her traditional school staff sent clear messages for appropriate teacher behavior, such as the janitor who forbade her to have a braid rug in her room. The same clear messages were sent to students, for example, by the principal, who flashed cafeteria lights off to modify the lunchtime behavior. Through reflection on her beliefs about learning, she was able to challenge her own assumptions and make decisions about which norms to challenge and which to work in more subtle ways. Only with some experience was she able to judge her work with a sense of ownership and responsibility.

Terry recalled more self-talk after the school year ended, valuing contact with each student:

> It felt like I was achieving what I needed to do. It felt much better looking at the kids as individuals, and with only 10 kids, I kept telling myself, "If I couldn't connect with each kid every day, I was nuts, what was wrong with me?"

Terry was well aware that her rural school class size was tiny, and that once in suburban school, she would be challenged to relate to 30 children. Again, the importance of making meaning of these first, tentative steps in a remote, rural setting with few children was evident to this new teacher, who would be required to transfer these understandings to a new school the following year.

How Do We Begin
to See Ourselves as Leaders?

Studies of professional induction teach us much about how newcomers find their way in a complex profession like teaching (Bullough, Knowles, & Crow, 1991; Ryan, 1986; Zeichner & Gore, 1989). We also learn about how we begin to see ourselves as leaders. If teaching is leading, perhaps new teachers can instruct us about the importance of personal development and self-knowledge for leaders. Many of the reflections by new teachers were about making sense of their novice status. Marilyn shared her thoughts:

> And here I am and I have to teach these kids, even though it's a small group, yet I felt, "I'm going to teach these kids, and I'm not ready!"

Marilyn definitely had the skills required to impart knowledge using traditional methods, but she had much less confidence about whether children would actually learn. Susan mused over her emerging relationships with young people from 13 to 18 years old:

> I was trying to find the continuum [of authority] of where I could be with them [high school seniors] and with my junior highers. I didn't feel like I could "come down on them" because I didn't feel like I was the expert in the class . . . there were so many factors."

Early in her first year, Susan recognized that, at 24, she was only a few years older than her students. What were the implications for her making sense of her role as teacher? Her mythic teacher model was described in a portrayal of a favorite teacher who was an older, male minister. For her, the choice to construct meaning together was a nonchoice. She couldn't be that older, wise man; she was almost a peer with her high school students. In Susan's case, her age and the social context of a high school classroom forced her to reconstruct her old myths about teaching.

All teachers, young and experienced alike, struggle to know enough to be "leading" learners. Outside the classroom, teachers find that people within and outside the profession seem to have expectations of them beyond what they might have for other professions. Within school, teachers' aides, nonteaching staff, and parents play a critical role in shaping teachers' beliefs about their abilities. Outside of school, community members, friends, and the media play an additional, if more abstract role, in reflecting back beliefs about the role of teacher. Barbara talked about her experiences in social settings:

> I'll be around people that aren't teachers, and they'll ask me a question about, "What's the highest mountain in a certain area?" and I can't tell them. They look at me like, "Well, you're a teacher." And I think, "Golly, what am I doing teaching? I should know these things."

The public nature of schooling allows anyone the freedom to judge teachers and leaves teachers vulnerable to anyone with an opinion about schools. Because the classic stereotype of teachers and leaders is that they should know all, they are not often invited to express ignorance or to engage in a type of learning that requires the public vulnerability that can accompany constructivism. If teachers allow themselves to feel victimized when others frame their roles, it will be hard to move toward more interactive ways of making meaning.

New teachers understand quickly that there is much to learn about who one is, how one teaches, and how much "content" each has yet to learn. How they choose to respond to their own learning becomes central to how they construct the learning environment for their students. For instance, if a new teacher has confidence that he and his students can participate together in new learning, new topics of study are within reach. If teachers are fearful about areas of little expertise, they may not seek more knowledge, with or without the students. A glimpse of this phenomenon can be seen in teachers' perceptions of literacy in language and mathematics. Most elementary teachers are confident about language and will experiment with creative constructions of meaning making, whereas in mathematics, a discipline described by many adults as a weak area, teachers tend to stay close to the text. The acceptance of constructivist methods of learning can create a culture in which professionals can say, "We can learn together!"

One place where teachers learn about not having "correct" answers is in their role as meaning makers. Meaning is made in relationship with others, and building such authentic relationships is central to success in constructivist leadership. In their descriptions of this role, there are clues about effective leadership in schools. Many of the new teachers' descriptions of their work are really descriptions of their relationships with their students. They are not describing management; they are describing "caring for" (Grumet, 1980; Noddings, 1984). They discuss their interactions with children as humanistic rather than bureaucratic or regulatory. The literature on teacher satisfaction cites positive relationships with students as a key element. According to Lieberman and Miller (1990), "The greatest satisfaction for a teacher is the feeling of being rewarded by one's students. In fact, most of the time the students are the only source of rewards for most teachers" (p. 154). Although these authors speculate that professional isolation or the need to be liked are reasons that teachers turn to students for feedback, perhaps the opportunity to construct learning together within a trusting relationship is a more positive spin on this professional dependence on students.

Susan described a boy whom she had confronted for some misdeed:

> I know this child was never disciplined in the traditional ways of being spanked or being told no. . . . He's a charmer, and I like him, but he doesn't see that because I make him do things he doesn't want to do. He sees me as someone real tough, mean. And at the same time, we have good eye contact: I know he likes me.

Susan's goal in this case was to provide guidance and set expectations, much as a parent would. She owns her responsibility to do so yet remarks on how the boy is relating to her.

Barbara revealed her thinking about the emotional development of a girl in her fifth-grade class:

> There are some kids in here, for instance Jessica, who is an individual thinker, but her individual thinking doesn't hurt other people in the classroom. She's not disrespectful of other people, so I admire her.

Barbara saw Jessica as an individual and as a member of a community of learners.

Marilyn talked about Hanna, a little girl who required special attention on an hourly basis:

> Well, she came to me in tears, "They didn't let me do anything. My brother never lets me do anything." Yeah, she never gets to do anything. She has older brothers. I said, "So did you tell them how you felt?" She said, "No." This child needs a hug and compassion, not lots of instructions.

Marilyn begins with the most basic needs of the child. These characteristics of "caring for" are important to relationship building, rather than problematic.

Much of the research on teacher development in relation to the client, or student, focuses primarily on the new teacher's ability to "manage" the classroom. This industrial image, one of patriarchal leadership, assumes a stance that teachers are middle management and students are workers on an assembly line. Indeed, one can peer into some classrooms, with their straight rows and dittoed worksheets, and choose the term *manage* without fear of misunderstanding. In these excerpts, however, new teachers were peering into mirrors of their own souls as they looked into the eyes of their students. In each student's journey, these teachers found a piece of their own story, and they drew on their own life histories to parent, guide, and counsel the children (Collay, 1988). In so doing, they found themselves healed from wounds that had occurred in their own lives as learners. Teaching and learning, especially in the constructivist philosophy, require dialogue (Freìre, 1970) and social interaction, requiring the whole person to enter the process. Only teaching that is telling allows the presenter the freedom of remaining distant.

Vygotsky (1962) and others have debated the nature of learning in schools, attempting to separate independent or innate learning from learning that occurs because of interactions with other children and adults. We believe that learning is interactive and that adults and children make meaning and construct knowledge as members in a community. The excerpts above demonstrate "teacher talk," or how young teachers made meaning of their interactions with children. Few people would call the act of empathizing with a 7-year-old leadership. Yet, if we recall the words of Rallis (1989) about the role of teachers as "catalyst, guide, interpreter, and facilitator for a process" (p. 201), there is certainly a purposeful dimension to the guidance of others. Teaching and learning with others is the setting in which young teachers make sense of who they are becoming as adults. They and the other members of their learning communities construct a time, a place, and a feeling about each other and about their sense of place.

Mature teachers not only demonstrate leading children by maintaining their focus on humanity, but they also move more boldly into the roles Rallis describes: catalyst, guide, interpreter, and facilitator. With maturity and sophistication, however, they interact with and influence the community of adult learners as well as the children in their classrooms. The second study that informs this chapter is a series of interviews with midcareer teachers who have completed a Master of Arts in Education. The geographic setting is the upper Midwest, with teachers representing districts that are urban, suburban, and rural. The average age of the participants is 40, and the group reflects the average American elementary schoolteacher: primarily white, female, and Christian. Their age is more telling than their years in service, because most are mothers who stayed home to raise children at some point in their careers. This degree does not lead to the principalship, so it tends to attract teachers who explicitly state that they have no desire to become principals. Yet their stories demonstrate tremendous acts of leadership in their schools—from the catalyst, guide, interpreter, and facilitator roles mentioned earlier to radical acts of disruption.

Experienced Teachers and Leadership

The new teachers in the previous study focused their learning primarily on students as individuals. Experienced teachers who choose more visible roles of leadership, however, speak more about interactions with colleagues, reciprocal activities, and seeking shared meaning or common purpose. The first experienced teacher presented here is Fran, an English as a Second Language (ESL) teacher in an urban school. Fran worked with non-English-speaking Southeast Asian kindergarten students. She became aware of her students' potential involvement with gang activity because her husband was on the police force, and she was very knowledgeable about the juvenile system. Fran researched her topic for two years, becoming an expert within her graduate cohort and her urban district. After she completed her thesis and the program, I asked her if she had presented her recommendations to her staff. She replied, "Not terribly much. I've done a fair amount with my own students here. Oddly enough, never to staff, never as a staff inservice presenter. I've done staff inservices with other buildings." When I asked her if she anticipated making more formal presentations of her work, she said,

> I've gone to see other staff. I gave a presentation at the TESOL [Teachers of English to Speakers of Other Languages] conference. I'm a member, and that one was kind of interesting because there was feedback that certainly our district should use new forms of teaching. I presented at the Hmong parents' meeting. But of course there's no money involved.

Fran's thesis was original, theoretically sound, and was the quality of a doctoral dissertation. Within her own building, however, she was not seen as an expert, at least not one that might conceivably be paid for her services. More important, she did not see herself as a leader. There are a few interpretations we can make here. One might be that Fran still sees herself as "just a kindergarten teacher" after many years in the same building. Teachers who teach the youngest children or those with disabilities—limited English proficiency is often categorized with other disabilities if one examines policy closely—have the lowest status in a school, and Fran may have internalized those beliefs.

Midlife female teachers who seek advanced degrees and remain in the classroom are seldom acknowledged for new expertise the way a teacher turned principal is. There are few visible turning points for midcareer professionals who remain in the classroom. District administrators, who spend great sums of money on outside experts, may not have the information about internal experts, and site-level leaders may not be socialized to advocate for teachers who may be more knowledgeable than they are themselves. Teachers who do serve in leadership roles without formal appointments (e.g., teachers on special assignment) do so at their regular salary, reinforcing the standard that only principals with licenses and formal appointments can be leaders.

Fran may have chosen not to make public her changing perception of herself from a teacher without remarkable special expertise to one who brings expertise to her school community. Experienced teachers develop areas of expertise, but the nature of the profession does not encourage formal dissemination of teacher knowledge. Teachers like to talk about new ideas with colleagues, but not at the risk of stepping away from the others by cloaking themselves in the mantle of expert. Teachers who are identified by principals as leaders or experts risk loss of association with peers and may find that the risk is not worth the acknowledgment. We believe that the pervasive "egalitarian ethic" (Lieberman, Saxl, & Miles, 1988) held by teachers and the culture of schools must be acknowledged and addressed in movements of educational reform. Fortunately, leadership as we have conceived it does not require expertise as much as it does mutual respect, listening, posing questions, and making sense of teaching together.

In addition to the school culture that rewards fitting in, school administrators have historically played a role in problematizing teacher leadership. For instance, in urban districts in Minnesota (and in many other districts throughout the United States), a role called Instructional Assistant has emerged in recent years. Teachers take on administrative tasks while retaining a regular teacher's salary. This is a place where teachers' unions might take a position on teacher leadership. The dilemma posed by this practice is that teachers need and deserve opportunities to practice roles of formal leadership, yet bureaucratic procedures cannot allow them the extra pay made available for administrators. This practice confuses our efforts to create opportunities for all members of the community to lead and to participate.

Another veteran teacher, Nancy, described her current role as a teacher of sixth graders in a suburban school. She had recently completed her thesis on gender equity in schools and remarked about that experience:

The master's program reawakened my interest, it rejuvenated my confidence, it allowed me to not just sit back and accept what people say and accept directives without really thinking about it. I'm interested in making some changes and raising awareness in other people, whether it be through workshop situations or through conversation, as well as in my own teaching.

Nancy's commitment to engage colleagues in a common purpose is evident in the following story. She and her colleague had designed a gender equity workshop for their colleagues, submitted a grant proposal to their district, and were asked to present their materials in workshops. In addition to making formal presentations, her informal behaviors had also changed: "I have aligned myself professionally with other people who are in the process of doing graduate work or who have just completed their graduate work." Her colleagues were people who were also active learners, rather than those who accepted things the way they had always been.

These veteran teachers have become expert in an area, owned knowledge of the broader profession, and still have not found the means by which to make a formal contribution in their own schools. The expectations they have of themselves, as well as the expectations of others in the organization, have limited their opportunities to contribute. It is important to many teachers to find entry points to participation through their expert knowledge. In the cases of both Fran and Nancy, experienced teachers with newly won knowledge have taken the first step in gaining expertise. Being knowledgeable, though, is not enough. Each must enter the next stage of development and reconstruct his or her professional image. Ways in which teachers can lead through their expert knowledge might include writing articles for local publications; teaming with a colleague to offer a workshop; working as alumni presenters in their graduate programs, where they offer credible role models to those who follow them; or developing courses and offering them in institutes or continuing studies courses. Thus, individual learning becomes individual acts of owning one's expertise through interactions with children and adults in settings such as these. Leadership processes can and should be shared and equitable, yet the skills of leaders include offering one's own knowledge to others. We believe that these intermediate steps may yet be necessary as teachers make the transition from "independent contractor" to member of a learning community. Formal knowledge acquired through graduate study was a key in their success at taking first, critical steps in efforts to become recognized as formal leaders.

Graduate education offers the safety of a learning community that may be less politicized and problematic than some school cultures. In addition to formal course work conducted seminar-style, which offers a culture of dialogue and shared colleagueship, students are asked and encouraged to present their new findings in formal settings within and beyond the academy. Publications of their work in newsletters and short articles for other members of the graduate program are supported. Thesis committees include an advocate or formal leader from the school site, so that each teacher has a link to the next stage of implementation. The importance of advocacy or mentorship for midcareer teachers cannot be overstated.

As we have described in the preceding chapter, the experienced teacher must work within a learning community in the professional setting of the school or district. Having acquired experience and knowledge, the community of the school is the place where new ways of practicing "colleagueship" occur. Teachers construct new knowledge with their peers, retaining what is good about their work and having the courage to introduce new ideas to old colleagues. This critical step doesn't happen easily. The constructivist approach to learning and teaching provides a more culturally acceptable way for teachers to lead. The learning community is the setting in which teachers and students are supported in their efforts to construct their own knowledge.

In this last example of teachers leading, a veteran teacher who chose to stay in the classroom has made the transition from informal to more visible leadership. Nina is a 24-year veteran who was on the design team that built her school in the late 1970s. Nina has welcomed and bid good-bye to several principals in that time and had been asked by her current principal to design staff development activities for her colleagues. This invitation followed several years of detachment from school activities as she completed her master's degree and during which school administrators had been perceived as ineffective. Nina's case represents the elements of constructivist leading presented in Chapter 2. She first outlined "the reciprocal processes that enable . . . " then created a series of conversations in which "participants in an educational community constructed meanings . . . " and finally, "led toward a common purpose of schooling."

Nina had invited Michelle Collay, the Director of Graduate Education at Hamline University, to work with her on a specific inservice activity for a staff just emerging from a period of frustration and disengagement caused by several changes in administration. This conversation took place one year after the inservice day that represented the beginning of a more active role as leader in her school. When Michelle asked Nina why the principal had engaged her to work with the staff, Nina described a principal who had "met with quite a bit of resistance initially. She's had negative feedback, defensiveness from staff members." Apparently, the principal's efforts to provide leadership had met with little success. Nina felt that teachers naturally resist change efforts from the top: "Plus, coming from the principal, it's different than coming from colleagues."

The inservice session she planned was an outgrowth of her thesis, planning a school structured around student happiness and a re-visioning of the school's mission. Teachers had become disillusioned with their status as a "reassignment school"—that is, a school into which students from across the district who weren't placed at magnet schools get placed. Michelle asked Nina to recall steps she had taken to prepare herself and Michelle for the professional development session to re-vision the school:

> I think I talked with people on an informal basis, passing in the hallway or whatever, finding out what issues were important to them. I think I even surveyed the staff, just a little piece to find out where people wanted to go, looking at some redirection. I think we even had some discussions at staff meetings and in other places. Prior to your coming, we did some preplanning to get a sense of what to do. And then Anne [the principal] had certain specific things in terms of our strategic school plan that we needed to incorporate.

We see in her language the tentative "I think." This represents an early stage of owning one's leadership, of choosing language carefully to retain her status as "one of the teachers," rather than a teacher who is becoming an authority, or a teacher who is aligning herself with ineffective administration. Although she was not as direct about owning the steps she took, she did express confidence about her ability to find out what her colleagues valued.

Nina and Michelle had talked about the importance of incorporating the school elders in the planning so that she would not be
isolated as a teacher leader and so that other senior teachers would
be honored for their historical contributions. Her next statements
reflect her careful efforts to create a map of the school history with
her colleagues (see Chapter 3, p. 52) to elicit their support and demonstrate her respect:

> I did some background research on the school; I pulled all
> those folders to get a sense of where we had been. One senior
> teacher and I talked about memories of the annex, the farm
> school. I talked to Linda, who I taught with when we first
> started. It was a country-type school; we ate lunch together
> in the office. When I started talking about this inservice with
> other senior teachers, they said, "Oh yeah, those were the
> best years of our teaching!" I think that really did help. I don't
> think they felt intimidated by their involvement with the
> session.

Applying her fine teacher skills, Nina perceived her role with colleagues as a catalyst or facilitator of their staff development activities.
She did not "carry the agenda" but rather solicited the hopes of others
in her community. Nina also talked about the collegial atmosphere
among the teachers, who could work well together and share ownership. At the inservice, she and Michelle modeled that approach as
they co-led the first session:

> In the morning, we [Michelle and Nina] worked as a team,
> so there wasn't just one of us hanging out there. In the after-
> noon, it was the same thing with Kathy and myself. It didn't
> feel like there was just one person saying this is the way it's
> going to be. I think that's a lot of it.

Nina felt that she couldn't "stand up in front" and instruct or give
answers to colleagues. She stated a value for a style of leadership
described by Robertson (1992) in her work on the role of gender in
leadership styles: "Women's leadership styles are expressed through
communication patterns which are more typical of collegial than
autocratic endeavors. Women's language patterns appear to create a

consensual and participative atmosphere for decision-making"
(p. 52). As a teacher and colleague, Nina was successful with this
approach to leadership.

This next reflection contains some of the reasons why Nina has
the ability to "evoke potential in a trusting environment." Whereas
the recent history of the school had been disrupted by mistrust, the
senior teacher group was credible and trustworthy. When Michelle
and Nina talked more about trust building and how she had earned
her status as senior teacher, Nina said,

> Longevity is part of it! One person said, "Go talk to Nina,
> because she doesn't just talk about changing something, she
> does something!" I think of the way I try to interrelate to the
> people in the building. I tell the truth, I'm respectful, I don't
> act like I know everything. And I've been here a long time. I
> came with the building! And professionally, I think I'm a
> good teacher. And I think other people recognize that.

As Nina reflected on the traumas of her teaching day with second
graders, she added ruefully, "Maybe not every day!" We talked more
about teachers who have longevity and experience but do not garner
the respect Nina was describing:

> There are people who have been in the building for a long
> time. They just kind of sit back and let other people do the
> work; they won't take a position on anything. They're not
> risk takers; they're not going to put their head on a chopping
> block or speak up at a staff meeting. They stick with the same
> old things; they won't try some new things. I think those
> people look at teaching as a job, rather than as a vocation or
> a blissful experience or what your journey in life is. And there
> is a difference!

In these remarks, we see evidence of the importance of vision for
anyone in a leadership role. Experience, longevity, and just knowing
the history don't seem to be enough. Having the courage to speak
her truth and to move toward a goal were central to Nina's perception
of herself as a leader. Michelle had talked with Nina about the context
of their interview being "constructivist leadership" and her belief

that teachers undertake approaches with children similar to those that good leaders take with adults. When she asked Nina, "If you were to put language on what you do with adult colleagues, what language would you use?" Nina answered,

> I'm real active in committees that make a difference in the building, committees that can get change going. I'm not afraid to say something in the staff room. I'm not afraid to take a stance, even though I have been in the past. I'm not afraid to shoot my hand up and say, "Hey, wait a minute. Maybe there's another possibility."

Michelle was curious about whether this more proactive stance Nina described was a recent thing. Nina said,

> It's been since I got into graduate school. Since I got into the master's program and began getting into all the information in education, and talking to people in other schools, it gives you a base of current knowledge. You ground yourself better, you come across as if you know something, and you question more.

Again, the role of graduate education for Nina cannot be underestimated. In a community of learners motivated by the same thirst for knowledge, Nina, along with Fran and Nancy, gained a level of confidence that translated into inquiry and action. We closed the session with a comparison of teacher leadership for children and for adults, something Michelle had asked Nina to think about at an earlier meeting:

> What do I do with the staff in terms of leadership? I do about the same thing I do in the classroom! That's what I do. You structure things for success, you interrelate to people in certain ways, you're positive, you try to facilitate them through where they need to go, you allow them leadership, you give them choices and options. If you really sat down and listed all the things you do with children in classrooms, if you're effective with kids, a lot of it is all there. It's just a different level.

There are two important and parallel strands to Nina's perception of her role as a "teacher who leads." The first strand is the importance of the credibility earned by her long-term membership in the school community. In the first part of her reflection, she revisits the history of the school, and her longevity is named as an important factor in her ability to lead. Other factors that are important include "I'm truthful, I'm respectful, I don't act like I know everything." Her stance allows reciprocal behavior to remain central to interactions and, therefore, offers potential for interdependence. These values that Nina states give her recognition and respect by others. She is a team player in how she hears what others have to say and includes them as equals. These characteristics are evident in classrooms designed for constructed knowledge and are central to the success of all members of the community. A teacher who values student confidence and success over merely completing basic assignments offers such a learning community to students. This learning community is holistic and open, not linear and closed.

Second, Nina states the importance of "voice." She is not afraid to "take a stance." This ability to risk criticism by others does not come early in practice, at least it did not for this teacher. Nina cites her graduate education as key to her confidence as a professional: "You ground yourself better, you come across as if you know something, and you question more." Each of us must feel confident that our voice carries weight, that we speak from a place of knowing, and that we can back our claims with real information. In the next chapter, we will more thoroughly discuss the issue of "voice" and its relationship to power and authority.

With the strength of credibility among peers, confidence in hard-won knowledge about the profession, and a sense of voice, what else is necessary for constructivist teacher leaders to succeed?

Conclusion

Teaching is an act of leadership, requiring an understanding of one's role, a commitment to empower all learners, the skills of facilitation, and the willingness to inquire about and reflect on one's own learning. Teaching and learning are highly relational, interactive, and grounded in the lives of the participants. Constructivist leaders are

teachers. Those who teach will recognize the following social interactions necessary for learning described by Wells and Wells (1992):

> Like the culture itself, the individual's knowledge, and the
> repertoire of actions and operations by means of which he
> or she carries out the activities that fulfill his or her per-
> ceived needs, are both constructed in the course of solving
> the problems that arise in goal-directed social activity and
> learned through interpersonal interaction. Human develop-
> ment and learning are thus intrinsically social and inter-
> active. (p. 29)

A constructivist leader recognizes and values this framework for
learning. From first-year teachers who are capable of leading children
through their learning and of constructing self-knowledge about that
leadership role, to experienced teachers who are skilled in their colleagueship with other adults, we have seen exemplary approaches
to leadership—if we choose to name what they do as such. As teachers make meaning with their students, they are participants in
the collaborative construction of knowledge. It is ironic that, even
though teachers' leadership is often dismissed as child care, we can
look to classroom teaching as a source for metaphors of the roles of
leaders. If we accept teachers as leaders, what can we learn from
teaching practice about leadership?

New metaphors for leadership are necessary. The term *constructivist leader* offers many possibilities beyond those we have inherited
from the patriarchy. Rallis (1989) believes that metaphors of leading,
which include "steward, captain, visionary, evangelist, manager, or
instructional leader are inadequate because they suggest leadership is confined to a role or described by a set of skills or tasks to be
accomplished" (p. 203). Teachers, as constructivist leaders of children's and adults' learning, can lend different metaphors for leadership. Their contributions, however, will not be embraced within old
paradigms of school organization. "The espoused theory of teacher
leadership would be undermined if theories in action stress teacher
compliance as opposed to creative risk-taking" (Cliff, Johnson,
Holland, & Veal, 1992, p. 906). Only when the school community
is itself a learning community as a result of constructed knowing

and shared meaning will the contribution of teachers be considered leadership.

Is it possible to imagine school communities where all adults teach all other participants in learning? Sacken (1994) calls our attention to the importance for school leaders to stay closer to children—and, therefore, to retain opportunities to construct meaning with all members of the school community: "People who want to contribute to the well-being and future of children simply must work with them. At the least, they should not be paid more not to work with them" (p. 669). The historic paradigm of stratified leadership is with us still. And the creation of new or different metaphors for leadership remains the challenge before us.

How we choose to practice leadership must relate directly to how we teach. Different models of leadership can be derived from teaching, and the role of leader will allow for many kinds of participants. In a collaborative process with colleagues studying the characteristics of constructivist leaders, we hoped to draw together the common traits between teaching and leading. We must look to our classrooms as the beginning point rather than as the end point:

> Our position is that for substantive and widespread change to occur, we must start with a vision of what we want to occur in classrooms and schools, and then begin to question which existing structures support or facilitate that image and which must be altered. (Cohn & Kottkamp, 1993, p. 260)

Teachers have much to contribute to our thinking about leadership and leading. The traditions of constructivist education offer a powerful catalyst for our thinking about the work of teachers and their roles as leaders. This conversation has always attracted people of many philosophies, but the voices of teachers are being heard above the din.

Who Sets the Learning Agenda?

Issues of Power, Authority, and Control

> Our use of sex, money, and power to find out
> and express who we are is but the sign of a much
> deeper longing for meaning and connection.
>
> *Alan Jones, Dean of San Francisco's*
> *Grace Cathedral, in* The Soul's Journey *(1995)*

THROUGHOUT OUR PRECEDING CHAPTERS, WE have discussed several ideas that are important to this chapter as well. We began with a review of the major context issues in society and in the profession that cry out for innovation and creativity. We described our interpretations of constructivist leadership and its role in improving conditions for learning in schools. We advanced a view of systems thinking that takes an ecological, constructivist perspective and that will assist constructivist leaders in establishing a culture for inquiry and learning in school systems. We also defined and presented portraits of learning communities in which teachers collectively participate in the construction of knowledge and practice. Finally, we drew on the experiences of teachers to discuss the meaning of leadership within the classroom context.

These ideas might remain on the pages of this book ("a nice place to visit, but I'll never be able to live there") if we did not address the dynamics involved when issues of power, authority, and control arise—which they surely do when fundamental change is undertaken in schools. Our purpose in this chapter is to reframe our understanding of power and authority from a view that is dominated by issues of authority and control *over* others to one characterized by facilitation, relationship, and participation *with* others.

To reframe these understandings, we will

- discuss current views of power and authority in our society;
- describe definitions of power and research that depict alternative dynamics of power in organizations;
- propose aspects of power in constructivist leadership that enable those in the community to take positive action; and
- describe some focal points for leaders to use in addressing power, authority, and control issues that may be currently present in schools and school districts.

Current Views of Power

Power is often a troublesome topic, seldom overtly discussed within the context of schools, perhaps because of negative, emotion-laden attitudes that accompany such discussions. Some of the foremost educational reform writers avoid the topic completely when writing about school change. Yet avoidance of the issue inhibits our ability to understand and reframe our conception and use of power within the organization, a necessary task for teacher leaders.

Generally, in our society, power is viewed negatively as characterized by domination, reduction of choices, and having power over others. Joanna Macy,[1] systems theorist and author, speaks to how our tendency to build defenses has become identified with power, creating illusions for ourselves that we are invulnerable. These defenses impede our ability to connect with one another for the sake of the common good. In addition, hierarchy armors us from one another in ways that make it difficult to be in relationship with one another. Often, this armor is displayed by words and deeds that express "I am so powerful that I will not change my mind." This type of power is inherently framed from a mechanistic perspective: This results in seeing ourselves as "things"—selling ourselves as "stuff," turning ideas into "stuff"—creating conditions in which we believe there actually is a fixed body of knowledge. This mechanistic view of ourselves and our ideas usually results in competition and manipulation. Defenses often arise in relation to myths.

Macy identifies six prevailing myths about power:

- Power is a scarce commodity, a zero-sum game, and only some people have it.
- Power and authority is vested solely in positioned leaders.
- For me to have power, I have to reduce yours.
- Power is forcing one's will on another and reducing choices for others.
- Building defenses makes us powerful.
- Having power gives one the ability to legislate meaning and fix identity.

These are the myths that teacher leaders must challenge if they are to save our schools. First, if change occurs because of people in power, then many people must be empowered. When students and teachers are feeling powerful in their learning—have greater competence and a sense of accomplishment—then schools will have made great strides toward reform.

If a condition of having power is that I have to reduce yours, then we may feel that we need to force our will on others and reduce their choices. This scenario of power over has been played out in schools for several decades. In the meantime, schools get worse. Even colleagues find themselves attempting to coerce or manipulate one another. The following scenario is drawn from an experience of one of the authors in a suburban middle school when an entire faculty had come together for a day to collectively generate a vision for themselves and their staff culture. The groups had engaged with one another all day to craft some working agreements they would commit to using. When it came time to come to consensus on the shared vision and commit to it, the following scene occurred:

Senior teacher: (standing up and speaking in a rather loud voice) This must be the 70th time we've papered these walls with chart paper filled with our ideas, but nothing ever changes. This is just a big waste of time. We've spent days and days *just talking*. I've been at this school for over 20 years and we've done this all before. I *resent* the idea that we need to change. This is all just so much BS.

Facilitator: How do the rest of you feel about this?

(Silence in the room. Finally, a teacher from another table speaks.)

Second teacher: (looking at the facilitator) You know, I'm new here. I've only been teaching at this school for 7 years, but you know, every time one of us new teachers expresses an idea or something we want to try, one of the senior teachers stands up and tells us "No!" I've heard this before. They say, "We've done that, tried that." That's why nothing ever happens here after these sessions. And I think that's wrong.

(Second teacher draws in her shoulders and hunches down in her chair, as if ready for something to fall on her. Silence descends on the room again for a minute or two.)

Second senior teacher: (looking at her senior colleague) You know, Betty, we do that. Maybe it's time we started listening and considering some of these ideas again.

In this moment, these senior teachers, who had been able to overrule curriculum or school structure changes proposed by less senior teachers or by the administration, were challenged through the courage of a less senior teacher. She gave voice both to her perspective on their relationships and to her ethical concern. More often, threats of intimidation and coercion by colleagues are effective in ending discussions of change because teaching cultures are characterized by strong norms to be congenial, interpreted as "being positive." Challenging one another is interpreted in such cultures as "being negative." This aspect of teaching cultures gives great power to those who would dare to intimidate others.

In cases in which teachers and students see themselves as victimized by the hierarchical system in which boards of education and superintendents act on positional authority, defensiveness in the face of critique or feedback will be the standard response. Resistance to change is often created when those in positional authority make demands without the benefit of engaging with those who work in schools and classrooms. Closing the classroom door has its advantages when the demands and requests from the system do not make sense; one can armor oneself to gain a sense of control over situations.

But what does that mean for students whose school experience is composed of classes taught by one teacher after another acting alone? The collective establishment of commonly held beliefs is critical to constructivist leadership, and teacher isolation does not permit the kind of collegiality required to construct anything.

If power and authority are vested in only a few people by virtue of their position or their ability to coerce and intimidate others, then the voices of those who do not see themselves in such positions will not be heard. For teachers, this raises a question of moral responsibility. David Steindl-Rast (Capra & Steindl-Rast, 1991) describes the issue in this way:

> Those in authority should use their power to empower those under their authority, to make them stand on their own two feet. To empower someone means giving them authority; and to give someone authority means giving them responsibility. That is why the coward in each of us doesn't want authority; we simply don't want the responsibility that goes with it. By shirking our own responsibility, we play into the hands of authoritarians. (p. 191)

If teachers are to save our schools, then relationships built on dependency in hierarchical associations must be changed to relationships that support greater resiliency and a greater sense of community. In Chapter 3, we suggest that self-organizing systems strengthen the capacities of communities to be resilient and sustainable. To make the transition from bureaucratic, authority-driven traditions, issues of individual power and authority will need to be surfaced and relationships realigned.

Dynamics of Power in Organizations

To develop a full understanding of power in organizations, it is helpful to examine various definitions of what we mean by power.

Definitions of Power

Finding a true definition of power in organizations is a tricky process. The *Random House Dictionary* (Flexner, 1987) defines power in 32 ways. Synonyms, according to this definition, are *capacity, energy, strength, sway, rule,* and *sovereignty.* Lee Bolman and Terrence Deal (1991), in their studies of many types of organizations (large/ small, government/private enterprise, for-profit/nonprofit, educational/business), offer this perspective:

> [Power] is usually seen as an attribute that individuals or systems possess—an attribute based on the resources that they are able to control. Power is discussed as if it were real, that is, it is seen as something that can be seized, exercised, or redistributed. But power, like many other organizational phenomena, is often ambiguous. It is not always easy to determine who has power in a given organization. How one goes about getting power is often unclear. It is sometimes even hard to know when power is being exercised. From a symbolic perspective, individuals have power if others believe that they do. (p. 206)

Bolman and Deal adopt the description of D. C. McClelland (1945) of the two faces of power: "The negative face is power as exploitation and personal dominance. The positive face is power as a means of creating visions and collective goals" (p. 206).

In her research on American corporate environments, Rosabeth Moss Kanter (1983) defined power as "intimately connected with the ability to produce; it is the capacity to mobilize people and resources to get things done" (p. 213). She connects power to innovation by saying that "innovation . . . requires that the innovators get enough power to mobilize people and resources to get something *non-routine* done" (p. 213).

Carolyn Heilbrun writes that "power is the ability to take one's place in whatever discourse is essential to action and the right to have one's own part matter" (as quoted in Dunlap & Schmuck, 1994, p. 235).

Power and authority are systemically related. There is power in authority and authority in power. Heifetz (1994) defines authority as "conferred power to perform a service" (p. 57). He makes two points in regard to this definition:

> First, authority is given and can be taken away. Second, authority is conferred as part of an exchange. Failure to meet the terms of exchange means the risk of losing one's author-

ity: it can be taken back or given to another who promises to
fulfill the bargain. (p. 57)

Heifetz implies, through this definition, that relationship and mutual
agreements are necessary to maintain authority. As we will discuss
more fully later in this chapter, there is power in networks and alliances in which relationships are nurtured and mutual agreements are
made.

Dunlap and Goldman (1991) add an important metaphor for
leaders to consider, that of *facilitative power.* This term "is rooted in
the kind of interaction, negotiation, and mutuality descriptive of professional organizations" (p. 13). Again, the necessity of relationship
and mutual agreements surfaces.

These definitions will be integrated with "domains" of power
below. In view of these definitions, what are some of the features of
power that can be put to constructive use by teacher leaders?

Research That Describes the Dynamics
of Power in Organizations

Kathleen Hurty (1995) conducted a study that revealed five dis-
tinctive elements of power employed by 17 female elementary school
principals of schools in a large West Coast school district. She gathered her data through observations and interviews of these women,
who were identified by their district as effective principals. They
represented diversity in their ethnicity, age, and years of experience.
The five elements of power are

1. *emotional energy,* a willingness to use, honestly and openly, a
   full range of emotions in their work with other teachers, students, and the community;
2. *nurtured growth,* the ability to nurture even small evidences of
   learning and development;
3. *reciprocal talk,* talking with, rather than at, others by listening
   to, and learning from, other points of view;
4. *pondered mutuality,* keeping others in mind in the reflective
   rumination used in making decisions; and
5. *collaborative change,* working with and involving others in the
   transformation of schooling. (p. 385)

All of these elements can be characterized as power *with* rather than power *over* others. Once again, we see the theme of relationships and mutual agreements emerge.

An additional perspective on power is offered by Lee Bolman and Terrence Deal in *Reframing Organizations* (1991). They describe eight forms of power that individuals and groups must have to be powerful within organizations. These forms emerge from the work of a number of social scientists who studied potential sources of power that "partisans"—those not in authority in organizations—use:

1. *Position power (authority)*. Organizational positions, or roles, are associated with certain kinds and amounts of formal power.
2. *Information and expertise*. Power flows to those who have the information and know-how to solve important and vexing problems. Shifts in the environment may produce shifts in power.
3. *Control of rewards*. People who can deliver jobs, money, political support, and other valued rewards can be extremely powerful.
4. *Coercive power*. Coercive power rests on the ability to constrain, to block, to interfere, or to punish.
5. *Alliances and networks*. Getting things done in organizations involves working through a complex network of relationships among individuals and groups, and this is a lot easier to do if you have friends and allies.
6. *Access to and control of agendas*. Two of the by-products of networks and alliances are access to decision-making arenas and the ability to influence the agendas in those arenas.
7. *Control of meaning and symbols*. Elites and opinion leaders often have substantial ability to define and even impose the meaning and myths by which a group or an organization defines who they are, what they believe in, and what they value. Viewed positively, this is the capacity of leaders to provide meaning and hope.
8. *Personal power*. Individuals with charisma, political skills, verbal facility, or the capacity to articulate vision are powerful by

virtue of their personal characteristics, in addition to whatever other power they may have. (pp. 196-197)

Bolman and Deal sum up their description of these elements by stating that "the presence of multiple forms of power constrains the capacity of authorities to make decisions" (p. 197); that is, they constrain "the capacity of authorities to make decisions" in traditional ways. So often, teachers who express their feelings of powerlessness are assuming they are not in the positions to make decisions that matter. However, as these researchers define and describe power for making things happen, we see that there are multiple avenues of access to power both in groups and individually.

Power in Constructivist Leadership

In this section, we will use the forms and elements described by these researchers as a basis for reframing thinking about the use of power and authority in schools. The following seven domains of power are accessible to teacher leaders who are willing to create the conditions for systemic change.

Domain 1: Power in Alliances and Networks

Hurty's (1995) "collaborative change" and Bolman and Deal's (1991) "alliances and networks" lend description to this domain of power in a system. A healthy, ecologically designed system—whether it is a classroom, a team of teachers, a school staff, a professional association, or a school district—requires the existence of a complex network of relationships and alliances among those who possess the expertise relevant to the task. Moving a school toward supporting and sustaining new practices and structures *requires* alliances and networks. The teachers who participate in such alliances and networks have access to, and a voice in the control of, agendas and the ability to help create meaning, hope, and a sense of common values within a community. This network of relationships becomes the life energy of the organization (information, knowledge, expertise, resources).

Networks and alliances can also produce negative effects as related in the following incident:

Relatively small changes that challenge the status quo can illustrate how informal power networks operate. In one high school, there was a discussion at a staff in-service day to create a 10 min. "brunch" period in the middle of the morning for the students. Most of the staff felt that the students would attend their next two periods in a better learning mode and it would give the teachers a chance to get a cup of coffee and "connect" with each other. Important information between teachers could be shared, joint plans could be updated, etc. This idea gained momentum as the day progressed and one of the staff called for a vote to start the process to put the 10 minute break in the daily schedule. The vote was about 75 percent positive.

Since this movement came from the staff themselves and the positive vote, the principal felt ready to get the necessary permissions to extend the school day by 10 minutes. To be certain he had the support of the staff, he sent a memo to the department chairs for each of them to double check with their departments that this was indeed something he should pursue. The informal power structure became ignited by the thought that this would add a number of hours to their teaching day over a year's time. The power brokers discussed it among themselves and then went about influencing the others. When the results were sent to the principal, 80 to 90 percent of each department did *not* favor the brunch period. The proposal was abandoned. (Kent & Gemmet, 1990-1995, p. 4)

In hierarchical relationships, the ability to resist change is often the only type of power individuals feel they have. These teachers most often use it as a defensive or protective device to preserve some sense of personal autonomy and to avoid being harmed. In this example, the students' voices and interests were eliminated from the entire process. They often are.

Domain 2: Power in Personal Commitment

Teachers who possess a sense of clarity, purpose, and personal vision in their work and who are willing to pursue deeper understanding and greater competence with others in their performance provide energy to the system. Personal commitment includes Hurty's (1995) element of emotional energy—that "willingness to use, honestly and openly, a full range of emotions in their work with other teachers, students, and the community." It also includes Bolman and Deal's (1991) category of "personal power." When we are connected with our own individual purpose in our work, that emotional energy sustains us personally in persevering toward that purpose. This energy is integral to a sense of personal power.

Traditional efforts to identify and support teacher leaders have relied heavily on teacher abilities in this domain. Vivian Troen and Katherine C. Boles (1995) conducted a study seeking new models of teacher leadership:

> In our sample, authority was not *given* to the teachers and none of the teachers had the advantage of positional power and established leadership roles. They had exerted their leadership in entrepreneurial ways beyond defined boundaries, and their projects involved school restructuring, collegial collaborations, parent/community outreach, and curriculum reform/research. (p. 366)

Troen and Boles identified nine characteristics common to this sample of teachers. Six of the nine were versions of personal commitment: (a) passion about the project they had initiated; (b) confidence in its importance to children and teachers; (c) clear vision for school reform; (d) persevering, willing to promote her vision until it became a reality; (e) undaunted by bureaucratic constraints; and (f) unafraid to tackle the system that didn't meet the needs of students (p. 367). We attribute three remaining identified characteristics—(g) mid-career, over 15 years classroom teaching experience; (h) regarded as excellent teachers by colleagues, administrators, and parents; and (i) professionally active (attending conferences, teaching and taking workshops and college courses, pursuing advanced degrees)—to domains to be discussed in following sections: "power in information and special knowledge," and "power in status and position in the school."

Reliance by the members of a school staff on one person's, or even a few people's, sense of personal power to change the system can be a setup for burnout or what Michael Fullan has called "moral martyrdom." For example, a few teachers agree to take on responsibilities involved in a particular project like preparing a funding proposal or other project tuned to schoolwide goals. When the rest of the staff assumes that those teachers will continue to be the "point people" and carry full responsibility for the implementation of project activities with no rotation of responsibilities, even the most energetic and devoted person becomes discouraged. If the staff is structured as a learning community, the development and implementation of programs involve everyone in sharing the commitment and responsibilities. Special roles are shared and rotated among many members of the system.

Personal commitment and emotional energy are like many other human characteristics in that one's greatest strength can also be one's greatest handicap. This energy can destroy relationships if emotions and identity needs usurp other powers of wisdom and thinking, causing one to become attached to a particular outcome or way of seeing circumstances, regardless of other people's perspectives on alternate routes to the same end. This leads to attempts to dominate—to exercise power *over* others—resulting in loss of trust from others. In a learning community, giving and receiving support and feedback with one another can help to balance this personal emotional energy.

Emotional energy and leadership shared among many individuals collectively provide the synergy for the organization to move ahead and increase opportunities for individual renewal. Resiliency, as discussed in Chapter 3, becomes another result of the learning community for both students and teachers. This collective energy is a critical piece of forming and sustaining relationships.

Constructivist leadership engages each person's emotional energy *while* interacting authentically and reciprocally with others. Such engagement involves not losing sight of purpose while being able to view many paths to achieve it.

Through a clear sense of moral purpose and ethical nature, teachers earn the respect of others as long as their behavior is consistent with their espoused beliefs. As Anna Richert recently suggested to a group of teacher researchers, "It is the difference between doing it right and doing what's right—a much harder path to follow." Following the path of what's right earns one respect from colleagues, lending greater power to one's voice.

Domain 3: Power in Nurturing Relationships and Growth in Others

Throughout this book, we have explored the centrality of relationships and collaboration to reform in schools. These factors are deeply related to personal power. Nurturing growth, as Hurty describes it, is an interactive relationship quality—working with, thinking with, planning with, and deciding with one another—while keeping an eye toward reciprocal growth and development that includes both children and adults. This includes the idea of facilitative power, as described by Dunlap and Goldman (1991) above as "rooted in . . . interaction, negotiation, and mutuality descriptive of professional organizations" (p. 13).

Cohn and Kottkamp (1993) have focused on the place of school-based inquiry in their quest to support teachers as they reform schooling, nurturing growth in others. Inquiry also helps counteract tendencies toward "groupthink"—unquestioning enthusiasm for and adherence to an untested set of practices or ideas. They describe this newly emergent role for teachers as one of "collective autonomy," where teachers "may determine common purposes and work as colleagues to achieve schoolwide aims" (p. 284).

> The image we have drawn of thinking individuals working in concert in turn suggests a fundamental change in the role of school administrators. In schools as centers of inquiry, teachers do not need bosses to tell them what to do; rather, they need facilitators, coordinators of resources, and group process leaders who will support their initiatives. (p. 285)

This belief demonstrates movement toward constructivist leadership and nurturing growth in others but still contains two roles: facilitators of adults and facilitators of children. Indeed, adults need to be both types of facilitators, for children and for each other.

The process of "reflective rumination," as described by Hurty (1995), is another factor in nurturing relationships and growth in others. This involves turning problems over and over in one's mind, meditating and scanning for insights. This idea builds on Donald Schön's (1987) concept of reflection-in-action, a necessary element in learning one's craft. Reflective rumination includes interaction with others as a part of reflection-in-action. Posing ruminations to others is a structure for solving individual and collective puzzles or problems. The resulting power comes from the fact that this process often serves a group need to establish common meaning and can result in learning for the whole community.

Constructivist leaders are powerful when they design and facilitate occasions in which staff members join together for inquiry, for learning and developing together, and for building on one another's special knowledge and expertise as prerequisites for action planning.

Domain 4: Power in Information and Special Knowledge

As we described in Chapter 3, the open flow of information is vital to self-organizing systems. Bolman and Deal (1991) point out that power flows to those who have the information and know-how needed by the group in developing its self-organizing capacities. Through the exchange of information within the system, the whole group becomes more powerful in its increased capacity to flex and change with the changes in the environment. This type of power is enhanced and supported by the elements described by Hurty (1995) of reciprocal talk, pondered mutuality, and collaborative change.

Reciprocal talk is one of the reciprocal processes of leadership that we have described. It is one means for communication, decision making, and building trust that can connect individuals to one another. Most frequently informal in nature, this type of talk is a way of exchanging information and perspectives with one another and constructing meaning and knowledge. Listening to others and speaking truthfully provides the flow of information and knowledge that enhances and sustains mutual learning and the development of shared meaning.

In hierarchical organizations of schools, classrooms, or district offices—where some voices are dominant and some are muted because of position or other status indicators—harboring information feeds resistance to change. In classrooms, it leads to student disengagement—a form of passive resistance. Reciprocal talk is essential in developing relationships that can be positively related to organizational change. Examples of this process that endorses and supports resistance include many "parking lot conversations," held after meetings and the official workday. This form of resistance most often results in static, unchanging conditions in which conflict among members hovers beneath a congenial surface. In ecological systems, where members are working *toward a common purpose of the whole system*, reciprocal talk becomes a flow of information that sustains evolutionary learning and growth in the organization, rather than stasis.

The participation of many leaders who can provide diversity of special knowledge and communication linkages within the system will help to create and maintain a healthy system. A healthy organization needs to be able to respond to the variety of influences from its environment. As we have noted, the more dense the network of relationships within the school—diverse leadership styles, cultural viewpoints, discipline knowledge—the greater the group's ability to respond, collectively, to change.

In Chapter 7, we will discuss the area of professional preparation and teacher knowledge in depth.

Domain 5: Power in Seeing Both the Forest and the Trees

Leaders who can represent various points of view expressed in reciprocal interactions with others in the system and reflect that back to the group serve a group need for collective meaning and shared understanding of the whole system. When broader perspectives are offered to others, there is greater opportunity for each individual to identify his or her own role in relation to the whole system. Sharing broad perspectives with others can lower stress for individuals when they have greater understanding of the dynamics around them. One teacher, reflecting on her participation in a teacher research group focused on whole school change, commented, "When I hear that others are encountering similar experiences to mine, I relax a little in knowing I'm not alone and begin to understand how things work in the bigger picture."

Leaders who help facilitate the information flow among school staff members, students, and with parents and the community also help to create a sense of common purpose and meaning for the whole system. These connections allow the group to share power by participating in the construction of meaning and symbols incorporated in the collective identity of the system. Students who are engaged in developing class goals, a class flag, and class rules are sharing power and responsibility for how they work together in that environment.

Domain 6: Power in Status and Position in the School

Roles such as school principal, dean, assistant principal, mentor teacher, counselor, and department chair provide those individuals with tacit permission and authority within the school to have a voice in certain arenas of school life that gets people's attention. In the classroom, the teacher possesses this type of status. Staff seniority can also lend status to an individual in the school.

Even though positions allow people access to and control of agendas and rewards, status and position alone do not provide individuals with enough power, as Kanter (1983) says, "to produce or to get something *non-routine* done" (p. 213). Constructivist leaders who have such roles in schools, classrooms, or districts can use their status or position to get the attention of others and provide space and time for the participation of many in the learning community.

Rewards and recognition are powerful indicators of organizational values. Those who possess power through status and position have the responsibility to facilitate roles and relationships that distribute rewards and recognition in ways that are congruent with the values and purposes espoused by the whole group. A systemic use of extrinsic rewards such as grades and merit pay must be examined for their congruence with the values of the learning community. Are these rewards providing support for a person's learning? Are they creating meaning and a sense of identity within the systems one is part of? Or are they creating conditions in which domination and control are suppressing individual initiative and personal responsibility? Again, power with rather than power over becomes a factor in thinking through how we use our status and positions of authority and allocation of recognition and rewards within the school and classroom. We propose that working in partnerships toward common goals is the task of constructivist leaders.

Domain 7: Power in Partnerships That Grow

Service to the group and partnerships are aspects of the power in collaborative change identified by Hurty (1995). In *Stewardship*, Peter Block (1993) describes partnership as "being connected to another in a way that the power between us is roughly balanced" (p. 28). Stewardship, in Block's terms, is "the exercise of accountability as an act of service, requir[ing] a balance of power between parties to be credible" (p. 28). By encouraging team building and other processes that help members to renegotiate relationships and create open dialogue, teacher leaders can create conditions for a balance of power. A balance of power leads to shared accountability. As Block asserts, it is "to do more than improve communication. It is to create a balance of power. Accountability exchanged in both directions. Demands and requirements flowing both ways" (pp. 28-29). These qualities are also contained in our definition of reciprocity, one of the themes of this book.

Constructivist leaders demonstrate abilities to be flexible, to confront conflicts, to keep the focus on shared purpose, to share responsibility, and to seek consensus in partnership with others in the community. These abilities represent the capacities for building trust and respect. In their case study of their schools' change process, Ann Gessert-Wigfield and Alan Vann Gardner (in press) found that having a voice in the ongoing operations of their school gave the group a greater balance of power, power with one another in community, andincreasing levels of trust:

> We have found that trust to voice one's ideas and willingness to listen and respect others' concerns have evolved with time and by having had opportunities to come together, both in team-building and decision-making experiences. A member of our staff noted, "Students, parents, and teachers who became involved in the goals [of the school] took more responsibility for their actions."
>
> We have found that not only does trust invite voice but that voice deepens trust. Upon being interviewed, one

teacher reflected, "The more individuals have a voice, the more that you find in common and that what emerges are the highest qualities of relationship, like honesty." (p. 19)

In this case, the risk a person feels when speaking honestly about ideas and feelings within the organization is rewarded when one is heard and responded to. Using one's voice is viewed as an asset to the organization and these honest exchanges help to develop partnerships that grow.

As we noted in Chapter 2, teachers who exercise leadership in these ways also share responsibility for initiating conversations with others, including the principal, that address ethical behavior and moral purposes that encompass diverse backgrounds, cultures, and perspectives. This means bringing discussions of power, agendas, and conflicts into the organization rather than leaving them in the parking lot or becoming silenced through intimidation. This means sharing responsibility for seeing that all who are part of the education process of students feel they belong in the conversation. They have a voice in deciding the school's agenda for action, and they are respected for the knowledge, expertise, and point of view they bring to the group. This means really listening to others and bringing a willingness to incorporate others' ideas with your own.

Those in formal leadership positions must help to facilitate these discussions. Without the principal's initial support, teachers become easily discouraged, lose energy, and often burn out, returning once again to closing the door to their classroom and taking up the struggle to meet the challenges brought there by his or her students alone. Teachers cannot wait for support; they need to clearly describe what support is needed and say specifically what it would look like in practice.

Focal Points for Addressing Power, Authority, and Control Issues

Embedded in these seven domains of power are some focal points for constructivist leadership. Encountering issues that grow out of the use of power and authority within schools demands that leaders possess some personal qualities, including the ability to surface and confront conflict.

Joanna Macy (1994-95), together with colleagues, offers some guidelines that constructivist teacher leaders might use when encountering conflicts over power, authority, and control issues both within oneself and with others:

1. Attune to a common intention.
2. Welcome diversity.
3. Know that only the whole can repair itself.
4. Learn trust.
5. Open to flows of information from the larger system.
6. Speak the truth of your experience.
7. Believe no one who claims to have the final answer.
8. Work increasingly in teams or joint projects serving common intentions.
9. Be generous with your strengths and skills.
10. Draw forth the strengths of others.
11. [Realize that] you do not need to see the results of your work. Actions have unanticipated and far-reaching effects that may not be visible to you.
12. Putting forth great effort, let there also be serenity in all your doing; for you are held within the web of life, within flows of energy and intelligence far exceeding your own. (p. 2)

Macy's guidelines are points of focus for individual reflection and conversations with trusted colleagues and friends. These personal qualities will be integrated into our discussion of the commitments, knowledge, and skills of teacher leaders in the next chapter.

One of the toughest issues in a profession built on hierarchy, yet having established equality among those at the bottom of the hierarchy, is the need—and the reluctance—to hold each other accountable for the quality of the learning experience for all inhabitants in the learning community. This is another important focal point related to power and authority issues in school.

Holding each other responsible is a difficult expectation, yet it must be confronted lest autonomy in schools result in self-satisfied settings organized around adult conveniences. When adults in schools and districts fall into the convenience trap, they establish practices, such as tracking, 50-minute periods (giving all of the disciplines their share of the time pie), and parent meetings at times when parents cannot attend, that are often destructive to other community members.

Linda Darling-Hammond (1993) points out that genuine accountability involves a commitment of the faculty to collective inquiry so that evidence is a regular part of continuous improvement. Furthermore, she reminds us that accountability requires the responsible exercise of authority. Teachers need to work closely with principals and others who hold formal authority to ensure that that authority becomes an enabler, allowing schools to

1. develop a shared vision based on community values;
2. organize for, focus, and maintain momentum in learning dialogue;
3. protect and interpret community values, assuring both focus and congruence with teaching and learning approaches; and
4. work with all participants to implement community decisions. (Lambert et al., 1995, p. 3)

Marshall and Hatcher (1996) propose what they refer to as "collaborative accountability" that means "encouraging the growth of colleagues and sharing in their successes but also 'calling the question' when performance is unacceptable" (p. 45). For instance, unacceptable behavior that interferes with learning in a community is defined within the work of the Career Development Reinforcing Excellence (CADRE) program of the Illinois Mathematics and Science Academy. It includes, among other things, a failure to demonstrate commitment to teaching within a constructivist framework.

Determining quality within a learning community is a central question for consideration—an inquiry that needs to be undertaken among teachers, administrators, students, parents, community members, and district office personnel. Holding each other responsible for the quality of learning in a community will make traditional evaluation a vestigial structure.

Surfacing and confronting conflicts is a third focal area for teacher leaders to prepare for. Conflict within a school community can be encountered from several sources:

Data and information—who has it, who doesn't, whether it's fact or only possibility

Conflicting interests—and the belief that the needs implied in both interests cannot be met

Structure and cultural norms—when time and space constraints do not allow for adequate dialogue, unwritten norms cause members to feel "in" or "out" of the workings of the organization

Relationships—misunderstandings, hurt feelings, "past history," judgments made about one another based on untested assumptions that cause tension, stress, and avoidance of one another

Values—belief that there is only one right way to be

Accountability—efforts to hold each other accountable for the quality of learning in a community

As we mentioned earlier, congeniality is a strong norm in many schools. School staffs, in particular, have difficulty conducting meaningful dialogues when no one is willing to name the conflict that sits in the middle of the room like the proverbial elephant. Surfacing and confronting conflicts is not a comfortable task to carry out, but not confronting them is enervating and results in loss of a balance of power among the group. Intimidation and coercion are powerful strategies for getting one's way if the group is unwilling or unable to confront conflict and build toward consensus. In the next chapter, we will discuss further what some of those abilities are.

Gary Larson drew a cartoon showing a group of funny-looking people milling about a room together under a banner that says "Welcome to the POTP Club." The caption reads "The annual get-together of the Part of the Problem Club." Just as those of us who work in schools are part of the problem, we are also part of the solution to problems. To the extent that we cultivate our own abilities to work with and use power and authority in collaborative ways that are consistently ethical in nature, we become part of the solution.

As we look outside ourselves for others to take responsibility or blame for situations, we become powerless and part of the problem. The origins of teachers' sense of powerlessness are hard to identify. Powerlessness resides in the minds of people who decide that because they are not further up in the hierarchy, they have no power. Sometimes school staffs are conscious of the power they use to block and restrain the system from moving. These are some of the effects of the power over assumptions within educational hierarchies that create resistance because they have the authority to control resources and rewards. Is changing the power structure the challenge, or is it recognizing and reframing our understanding of the use (and misuse) of various forms of power?

Constructivist leaders will know how to help people create, articulate, and hold a vision of common purpose and shared goals. This involves understanding one's own part in the whole, establishing trustful relationships, and holding conversations in which operating beliefs and assumptions are surfaced. These beliefs and assumptions, including the frames we hold around power, authority, and responsibility, create our perceptions of the world.

Our thesis in this book is that teachers who become constructivist leaders will save our schools for our students and generations to come. Within the education system, there are people working in institutions and programs who can assist and enable teachers to become skillful leaders. In the next chapter, we will address preservice and inservice preparation of teachers who will exercise constructivist leadership in their schools and classrooms in ways that help to bring about the balance of power among individuals that propels schools toward becoming empowered learning communities.

Note

1. Joanna Macy, PhD, is a systems theorist and author who teaches at the California Institute of Integral Studies in Berkeley, California, and at Starr King School for the Ministry, also in Berkeley. This material was presented in a seminar on power as part of a series of ecoliteracy dialogues at the Center for Ecoliteracy, Berkeley.

Preparing the Constructivist Teacher Leader

WHAT KINDS OF LEARNING EXPERIENCES WOULD equip a teacher with the knowledge, skills, and commitments of the teacher leader we have described in the preceding chapters? We can begin by situating ourselves at the intersection of school reform and professional development reform. In recent years, scholars of school reform in the United States have placed teacher learning at the center of the reform agenda (Darling-Hammond, 1993; Darling-Hammond & McLaughlin, 1995; Little, 1990; Sykes, 1996). For schools to change, teachers need to imagine and enact the work of schooling differently. They need to have the time, opportunity, and capability for working with their adult colleagues to examine schools as they are, imagine how they might be, and work toward re-creating them in that new image. In this process of change, teachers will learn to teach different things and teach them differently. For teachers to change, the same logic holds: Professional education needs to provide different content and provide it differently.

Schools need to change so that they can better meet the needs of more children; few would argue that point. In the past several decades, the demands of an industrial society have given way to a technological society that is characterized by uncertainty, complexity, and change. Similarly, our social system has become increasingly complex, with changing demographics and changing technologies (involving how we communicate with one another) and so forth. The outdated school agenda of preparing predictable groups of people for predictable work is vanishing. What is emerging is an agenda of preparing changing groups of people to understand multidimensional—and changing—problems that face them every day. We must learn to frame and reframe these problems in new ways and to search for solutions in new ways as well. We must also learn to manage demanding, uncertain social and technological systems that require searching for new understandings and constructing new meanings. We must also learn to cooperate in building a flexible, dense, and powerful set of networks that can help us respond to the changing realities of the world in which we live.

Preparing Teachers
to Be Leaders of Change

Linda Darling-Hammond (1993) offers the frame of "capacity building" that includes the "capacity for leadership" we are positing as the centerpiece of this text. Building capacity is a useful construct for focusing our consideration of professional development in the context of change. Rather than developing a top-down system of direction and control to ensure school, student, and teacher success, Darling-Hammond suggests that we work to develop a capacity for managing uncertainty. As we learned from the discussion of systems thinking in Chapter 3 and of learning communities in Chapter 4, building capacity involves building an organization's ability to respond to changing circumstances while continuing to move toward common purposes. Organizations that are characterized by a dense network of relationships in which leadership is shared are more resilient to changing circumstances; they therefore have a greater capacity for change than those structured in traditional ways. Learning to lead in those settings requires learning how to frame and reframe problems, to search for more powerful solutions, to ask new questions, and to construct new meanings and methods that correspond with changing realities. Chapter 6 also claims that creating capacity requires naming and dismantling traditional authority structures and replacing them with a leadership structure that is as multiple and complex as the changing world it is meant to affect. According to Darling-Hammond, "capacity building requires different policy tools and different approaches to producing, sharing, and using knowledge than those traditionally used throughout this century" (p. 754).

The approach to professional development that we will present and exemplify in the following pages is directed toward building capacity by preparing people for school leadership in the context of change. Because it is contrary to constructivist thinking for us to argue that professional preparation occurs in one particular manner or another, we present instead an approach to professional development that is meant to guide the establishment of particular programs at particular sites. The approach we will suggest draws together the stance we have taken thus far on matters of teacher learning: (a) the context of that learning, which we have argued is collaborative relationships (collaboration), and (b) the mechanism by which that relationship is generated and sustained, which we argue is teacher *leadership.*

Professional development aimed at preparing teachers for their constructivist leadership role must be constructivist itself in both content and process. This entails providing teachers with the time, opportunity, and expectation to work with their colleagues in critically examining the important matters of their work—teaching, learning, schooling, subject matter, and school. This examination of the practice of their classrooms and their schools renders teachers lifelong learners who are constantly and consistently constructing new meanings that will guide future practices. Because this reflective examination of practice occurs in the context of collaborative relationships, it is important that teachers learn the skills of participation as a group member and/or leader. The teacher's role vis-à-vis this collaborative conversation depends on the demands of the task as well as the strengths, knowledge, and capability of the teacher leader.

Professional development for the teacher leader needs to begin in the teacher's initial teacher preparation experience at the university and continue throughout his or her career. Given that learning is at the core of both teaching and learning to teach—a point that is well established throughout this book—factors that enhance adult learning are vital to successful and effective professional development. Teacher learning in complex settings (such as the setting of school) where purposes, procedures, and problems change is characterized by a number of factors that can guide our thinking about professional development. These characteristics are drawn from our growing understanding of constructivism and reflect how we think about both teacher knowledge and about how teachers come to know:

- Teacher learning occurs as teachers engage in the reflective examination of the immediate matters of their work in school.
- It is an active rather than passive process—one that engages teachers in the active process of inquiry into the uncertainties of practice.
- Teacher learning is social rather than solitary; it is accomplished when teachers (and other adults) draw on their own past knowledge and experience as they work with others to examine practice and reach toward new understandings.
- Rather than moving toward the acquisition of some predetermined, externally defined outcome, teacher learning is seen more as invention or discovery. Teachers construct new knowledge that then raises new questions, which leads to further inquiry. This leads to a learning stance toward learning to teach.

The idea that teachers learn in collaboration with others is central to this model of constructivist teacher learning. It is drawn from two separate sources: (a) from constructivism itself, which defines learning as the social construction of knowledge and (b) from naming the *content* of that learning, which is the uncertain, complex, and changing world that teachers need to learn about. Collaboration as a methodology for learning has several characteristics that also inform our emerging model of professional development:

- Collaborative learning is powerful because the subject of that learning is sufficiently complex to warrant examination from multiple perspectives.
- Given that its strength is drawn from a multiple-perspective examination of practice, learning is enhanced when care is taken to include difference (diversity) in the collaborative conversation. Difference in this regard suggests crossing traditional boundaries to ensure multiplicity of perspective. Depending on the content of the matter under consideration, collaborative learning groups ought to cross grade levels, subject areas, role categories (teacher, administrator, novice, veteran, parent), and so forth.
- Collaborative conflict is an anticipated outcome of structuring collaboration to include difference. Conflict that can be

negotiated within the context of the collaborative conversation enhances learning.
- Collaborative learning requires having a nonhierarchical authority structure in which power and leadership are shared and conflict can be resolved within the context of authentic rather than role relationships.

Preparing the teacher leader to lead in reforming this world of schools requires that we create a professional development approach that incorporates new understandings of leadership as well. In recent years, we have seen a shift in our understanding of leadership and school reform. In the early years of the current reform movement, teachers were called on to serve as leaders of school change. The challenge for professional development was to prepare teachers with the capabilities for leading. However, because leading was traditionally conceived, the professional preparation was traditional in form. Teachers were taught to run meetings, have predetermined outcomes, and keep people on track. As our conception of leadership evolves toward a constructivist model that links leading and learning, so too must our plan for preparing teachers evolve. Several characteristics of constructivist leadership help us imagine how teachers can lead and how professional education might help them learn to do so:

- Constructivist leadership is reciprocal and happens in community. The role of the leader in this context is to create and sustain the occasion for other people to learn.
- Given its reciprocal nature, constructivist leadership is nonhierarchical. Depending on the problem at hand, the teacher leader assumes leadership responsibility based on his or her knowledge or expertise—rather than by assigned role in the school organization.
- Leadership, therefore, is contextual. Each context is different from the next, and the requirements for leadership—who should lead, how leadership should unfold, toward what end the process should be directed—depend on those differences. Contextual leadership helps both the leader and those in the collaborative group manage the uncertainty inherent in their task.

The Substance of Professional Development for Teacher Leadership

The next step in conceptualizing the professional development component for teacher leadership is to consider what the teacher leader needs to know and be able to do. Even before considering this, we must consider how the teacher views teaching and the set of commitments he or she brings to the work.

A teacher's work is framed by the view he or she holds about what teaching is and what schools are for. It is a significant paradigm shift to expand the role of teaching to include work beyond the classroom. We are discovering that this shift is a difficult one to make. Most teachers continue to see themselves as classroom-bound despite the reform rhetoric that has them valiantly leading the national school change effort. They themselves were taught by teachers who maintained a classroom focus, and they continue to be taught by teacher educators who are slow to reconceptualize the work as well. Such a change in conception requires a change in focus and a change in commitments related to that focus. These new commitments include serving the school and community as well as serving the children and parents at the classroom level. Clearly, this change also requires the acquisition of new knowledge and skills.

The challenge is how to prepare the teacher leader with these requisite commitments and skills, as well as the needed knowledge. The reform initiative in this country has conceptualized teachers as leaders in the reform process but has provided little guidance as to what that leadership entails and how teachers can be prepared to lead. Drawing on the conceptualization of the teacher as constructivist leader posited in Chapter 2, we turn our attention now to the question of preparation. In turn, we will focus our attention on commitments, knowledge, and skills.

Commitments

The work of the constructivist teacher leader is done in collaboration with other adults. As we have noted, this notion of collaboration represents a fundamental departure from the traditional role of teachers; a new set of commitments is required. The first one that we will consider is the commitment to collaborative work. Teacher leadership involves collaboration; teacher leaders collaborate with both children and other adults to solve problems, to construct knowledge, and to make decisions. They see themselves as part of a system of interconnected networks in which school people work together in an interdependent way toward the health and survival of the system as a whole (as well as the health and survival of the participants). Because teachers have traditionally worked in isolation from one another, establishing this commitment to collaboration (including both an expectation for, and value of, working with one's colleagues) is essential.

One step toward building a commitment for collaboration among school adults is to recognize the inherent uncertainty of teaching and school life. We argue here that schools are uncertain places where there is as much unknown as there is known about what can, does, and ought to occur. The situated nature of learning provides a series of examples that underscore the inherent uncertainty of the work of school. Situated learning means that how learning unfolds in any particular situation is different from how it unfolds in other situations, because learning depends on a number of contextual factors that frame the situation in the first place. What is true for one learning circumstance may not be true for another. For example, we understand from research on learning that learning mathematics is different from learning social studies is different from learning English and so forth (Ball, 1987; Grossman & Stodolsky, 1995; Stodolsky, 1988). Similarly, we know that learning at one grade level is different from learning at another and that learning in one school may require systems that are different from another.

As we have already argued in Chapter 1, despite our knowledge that learning is context-bound and that schools necessarily change in response to the changing contexts in which they exist, there continues to prevail a drive toward creating an image of school as a certain place, where people can and ought to be controlled and outcomes can and ought to be predetermined. Most people who have spent time in schools recognize that schools are not so controllable—nor should they be. The value of collaboration is underscored in an environment where people share ideas and work together to understand their complex and changing world. When more than one person is responsible for a program and its outcomes, the chances for successfully meeting the challenges of change are enhanced.

This conception of schooling as changing, uncertain, and complex suggests several additional commitments or dispositions as critical for the adults who work there. For instance, the constructivist teacher leader must be committed to continued learning. A learning orientation toward teaching includes approaching tasks in new ways, attempting to bring about different results. It also includes accepting less successful outcomes as an opportunity for growth. Taking risks becomes part of the teacher's commitment to grow as does inquiring about the outcomes of those risks. Teachers who are learners recognize that there is not one right way to teach or one set role for the teacher in school settings; they see themselves as involved in constant growth and change, which they do in collaboration with colleagues invested in creating learning communities directed toward accomplishing similar goals.

Creating a community of learners among teachers involves supporting both the risk-taking behavior of one's colleagues and the learning that is associated with that process. Both acts of support are predicated on commitments associated with leadership. More than a decade of research on learning has convinced us that learning occurs most powerfully in social, rather than solitary, settings. The commitment to learning that we see as central to the leadership role of teachers has collaboration as its corollary. Commitments to learning and collaboration carry with them a value for multiple perspectives. Learning is greatly enhanced as learners are challenged to think in new ways, consider different perspectives, articulate what they believe to be true, examine their beliefs in response to alternative conceptions, and so forth. For example, a characteristic of school organizations building the capacity for change, according to Darling-Hammond (1993), is that they value multiple perspectives and call for different voices to create a collaborative learning environment at the school.

As vital as these multiple-perspective conversations are for learning, however, they are difficult as well. This difficulty underscores the importance of building a commitment to multiple perspectives into teacher preparation. As teachers come together to discuss the issues they care about most deeply—teaching, learning, children, school, community—they bring with them many different points of view and values. And the intensity of their beliefs and values about these important matters causes the potential for conflict to be high.

Because dealing with conflict is difficult, it is important for teachers to recognize the connection of both conflict and multiple perspectives to learning in teaching. A critical piece of preparing teachers to be constructivist leaders of change is establishing the commitment to collaboration (albeit characterized by the presence of multiple perspectives and inevitability of conflict).

Knowledge

Let us consider next what teachers need to know to function as leaders in school settings. For the sake of simplicity, we will focus our discussion on knowledge domains that are needed to extend the teacher's work beyond its classroom-based beginnings. It is important to note in making this distinction, however, that the teacher's knowledge of children, subject matter, curriculum, and instruction are essential to his or her capacity for leadership; and it is because of this knowledge that we need teachers to provide leadership in schools. We rely on physicians to direct the work of hospitals (although we turn to hospital administrators to run the facilities), and we rely on ministers to guide the work of the parishes where they preach. In the same way, we are suggesting that teachers guide the work of schools and therefore function as leaders in those settings. The question then is—what do teachers need to know to accomplish this work?

In our discussion of commitments and teacher leadership, we discussed the centrality of the teacher's commitment to learning and to the creation of learning communities for both adults and children in schools. Consequently, an essential piece of the knowledge base for teacher leadership is knowledge about adult learning in school settings. There are several aspects of adult learning in this setting that warrant consideration: (a) the role of learning, (b) the constructivist approaches by which adults learn, and (c) the ways to provide learning opportunities for adults in school. Much of our earlier discussion about the changing, uncertain, and complex world of schools applies to our consideration of the role of learning for the adults who work there. We raise this issue again about the role of teacher learning because of how infrequently teachers are seen as learners (or as acquirers or creators of knowledge). In American schools, teachers are seen primarily as dispensers of knowledge rather than as creators of it. We can see how limited and limiting this image is given the uncertain and changing nature of the society and schools and how crucial is the need for learning in those complex settings.

The approaches by which teachers learn are embedded in the model of reflection and action posited by Dewey (1933) generations ago. According to Dewey, teachers learn as they consider current experience in light of prior knowledge and beliefs. This reflection on experience, in which teachers try to make sense of their experiences, leads teachers to construct new knowledge that will guide future actions. Recently, we have come to understand that this learning occurs best when teachers do this reflection together. Just as knowledge is socially constructed by children, it is socially constructed by teachers as well (Lambert et al., 1995). Teachers learn about teaching, learning, children, schooling, school change, community building, and so forth as they reflect with others on their experiences in the classrooms, schools, and school communities where they work. The methods of inquiry that frame the social learning opportunities for teaching are therefore part of the knowledge base of teaching—especially for teachers who will participate in creating those opportunities for others with whom they work. What opportunities are possible, how to establish and nurture them, and how to insist that learning be part of the work of teaching—these are all part of the knowledge base of constructivist teacher leadership.

The role of learning in teaching carries with it the idea of change. As people and organizations learn and grow, they change. Knowledge of change—what it is, how it functions in school settings, how it might be directed—is also a knowledge domain of teacher leadership. Throughout this book, we have established the inevitability of change and also expounded on the virtues of change in a healthy school environment. We argue here that knowledge about change is especially necessary given the current climate of reform that characterizes the national discourse on schooling. Teachers need to know about teacher leadership, about how teachers have participated as leaders of change in particular, about what factors promote and inhibit change in school settings, about the role of district and state policy in change, and about initiating and sustaining school change efforts (Fullan, 1993; Lieberman, 1995; Sarason, 1993; Wasley, 1993). An important part of the knowledge base for teachers in their emergent leadership role is learning about change, especially as these change factors connect with the overall learning agenda of schools.

This consideration of change in school settings raises the significance of organizational knowledge (or knowledge of the school organization) to the knowledge base we are framing here. The classroom-based work of teaching does not exist independent of its school and community context. Interestingly, teachers have functioned for generations separated from one another and from the decision-making processes that directly affect their work. As we understand more about how people learn, and about how the relationships and systems that connect us are critical to our lives and the lives of our organizations, we begin to recognize the cost we have paid for the separation and isolation of teachers in school settings. Schools are not neutral places; our examination of the cost of isolation and separation has revealed the political nature of schooling and the political reality of the school organization itself. For example, teachers who are separated from one another hold much less power in a zero-sum power organization than teachers who are united. Not only that, but teachers who are isolated are those who are most likely to leave the system either through burnout or dropout. Until now, many teachers saw the oppositional role of unions as the only viable united stance. When teacher leaders understand the patterns of power in school organizations and the relationships between sources of power, such as resources and knowledge, they can better understand the ways in which the larger school agenda affects the work of teaching and learning in their classrooms. They can better understand that when teachers learn together and work toward common purpose, schools and professional lives improve. Knowledge of change, school organization, and the politics of schooling are all necessary for teachers who lead.

Finally, knowledge of leadership itself is important. Along with changes in knowledge about learning for both children and adults, changes in conceptions of leadership are also emerging in the literature in education (Bridges, 1992; Bridges & Hallinger, 1995; Lambert et al., 1995). Teachers who are leaders need to know about both traditional and changing models of leadership. They need to know how the organizations pattern leadership and how the generation and support of ideas can be nonhierarchical despite the hierarchical organizational system of which they are a part. Similarly, they need to understand nonhierarchical organizational models in order to move toward replacing unsuccessful systems of management to meet the needs of changing times. Constructivist teacher leaders also need to understand the relationship between leading and learning and the relationships between the various interdependent parts of the learning system that is the context for their work.

Skills

Teachers who are committed to school leadership as part of their work in schools and who have a base of knowledge to support that commitment must also cultivate a set of skills that will allow them to do that work well. Believing that teachers ought to share in the leadership of schools is one important step that teacher leaders must make. Acquiring the knowledge about leading, learning, school organization, and change is another. But unless teachers are prepared with the skills that will allow them to use their knowledge to enact their commitment to lead, the chance for failure in their leadership roles is high. The research on teacher leadership and school reform bears this out in painful detail (Fullan, 1993; Glickman, 1993; Weiss, 1995). Let us consider, then, the skills that are essential for teachers to be successful in their leadership role in school settings. We have clustered the skills into three groups and will discuss them in turn: (a) collaboration skills (communication, negotiation, conflict resolution), (b) learning skills (reflective inquiry in both formal and informal ways), and (c) community-building skills (outreach, boundary spanning, organizing).

COLLABORATION SKILLS

Teachers who lead need to know how to collaborate. Ironically, although current thinking in education places considerable emphasis on preparing children to work and learn together, little is done in educational settings to help teachers develop those same skills. To start, teachers must learn to communicate effectively; they must learn to speak with confidence and listen with attention. These skills are not necessarily easy for teachers who are traditionally isolated from one another. Many teachers with whom we have worked say they have had surprisingly little experience talking about their ideas, beliefs, and practices with other teachers; nor have they had practice listening to their colleagues talk about these matters in turn.

Speaking and listening in professional settings are acquired skills that require preparation and practice. We find that this is especially so given the complex, uncertain, and often controversial nature of what teacher leaders typically need to talk about. In the context of reform, teachers are being called on to talk about the purpose of school, about children, change, diversity, the nature of learning, and so on. Each topic (and the many related to it) is multidimensional, complex, and often controversial. If the conversation were about less controversial matters, such as the deadline date for final grades or the monitoring schedule for watching the halls (as it was for so long in the history of teaching), the need for the communication skills of careful speaking and active listening would be less urgent. Fortunately, we are finally calling on teachers to share their knowledge and wisdom about teaching, learning, schooling, and children. To do so effectively, they need to know how to talk with others and listen when others talk with them.

The talk that engages teachers often leads to action. Because neither talk nor action is neutral, however, the communication skills needed by teacher leaders quickly expand beyond speaking and listening to negotiating and resolving conflict. When teachers and other adults with different perspectives come together to talk about issues that matter, they usually bring differences of opinion that require negotiation. Conflicts arise that need to be resolved. As teachers practice the skills of speaking and listening in the fray of conversation, where opinions vary widely, they need to know when and how to negotiate differences and how to move through conflict to resolution and action. They must be knowledgeable about the potential value of conflict for learning and committed to the inclusion of multiple perspectives for understanding the complexities of school life. With this knowledge and commitment in place, teachers can then develop the skills that will allow them to communicate and collaborate powerfully.

LEARNING SKILLS

Powerful collaboration results in powerful learning. As schools grow, change, and become more responsive to the society and to the communities they serve, they function as learning contexts for the teachers, students, and others who inhabit them. With learning as the central function of school, schools and their inhabitants have the capability to change; learning is the method by which change occurs. However, more often than not, learning is not seen as part of teaching; nor are the skills of learning inherently part of a teacher's work repertoire. The centrality of learning to teaching as well as the skills that are necessary to accomplish it must be part of the teacher education curriculum. Teachers must know what questions are important to ask; they must learn how to frame questions, search for evidence, analyze data, draw conclusions, and determine action. They must have ample opportunity to learn these skills and practice them in context.

These skills of reflective inquiry, which can be incorporated into both the teacher education course work and fieldwork, are based on an assumption that the work of schools is uncertain. If the work of teaching is seen as extraordinarily complex and uncertain, as we have posited it is in this text, then teachers must be positioned and prepared to examine the circumstances of their work before determining what actions they will take. They must learn to examine what they see and experience to understand it more fully. With the capability of understanding what *is* in the work of schools, and the capability of casting that against what *ought to be*, teachers are positioned to act with intent. This reflective process builds capacity for both leadership and change. And because learning is social rather than solitary, teachers who are learners actively participate in the conversations that lead to learning and thus to change.

COMMUNITY-BUILDING SKILLS

This brings us back to the importance of good speaking and listening skills. It follows that teachers who are leaders must also know how to create the occasion for effective speaking and listening to occur among the adults in their school community. This skill for teacher leaders is the skill of building community. It involves reach-

ing out to others to create the occasion for the conversation and to
determine others to reach out to ensure representation and richness
in the learning conversation itself. Thus, an important part of community-building skills is the ability to organize collaborative conversations.

These collaborative conversations are facilitated by the teacher
leaders' knowledge of the relationship between learning and change,
and their knowledge about learning itself. The skill of organizing the
collaborative conversation begins by drawing on one's knowledge of
what to organize for, whom to bring together, and how to facilitate
once the collaboration begins. We have presented leadership in this
text as a corollary of learning: The teacher leader creates the occasion
for others to learn.

Design Principles
for Professional Education

We are now ready to consider designing a program of teacher
education that would prepare the constructivist teacher leader. As we
argued above, the approach to professional development that we will
present and exemplify in the remaining pages of this chapter is
directed toward building capacity by preparing people for school
leadership in the context of change. Given the knowledge, skills, and
commitments we have just described, as well as the uncertain and
changing context of schools in which this leadership is to take place,
we are directed toward a set of principles that can guide program
development. Let us consider what these principles might be and
then what they suggest for the structure of teacher education.

We can begin by examining the timing of teacher education:
When in a teacher's career should professional development occur?

> *Principle 1:* Teacher learning is a lifelong process that begins
> at the preservice level and continues throughout the teach-
> er's career. The uncertain context of teachers' work renders
> learning a lifelong corollary to teaching.

According to Donald Schön and others who have written about professional practice and professional preparation in uncertain times,

teaching, like other professions attempting to serve the needs of a changing world, is confronted by the limits of technical rationality for understanding current problems; purely technical and rational approaches are inadequate for solving the changing and complex problems of practice (Schön, 1983, 1987). Rather than rely on accomplishments and lessons of the past, teachers must embrace a learning stance toward teaching that places inquiry and learning as centrally important to doing the work well. It is true that beginning teachers have considerable technical information to learn when they enter the profession, including knowledge about learning itself, about children, subject matter, schooling, change, and so forth. The agenda for preservice teacher preparation is considerable and broad; however, learning in teaching does not end when a teacher completes the preservice piece. The uncertain and changing world of children, society, subject matter, and school creates a condition whereby all teachers are learners for a lifetime. Teacher preparation must begin by preparing teachers for that approach to their work. The knowledge, skills, and commitments of reflective practice that this entails must be the centerpiece of teacher education at the preservice level and beyond.

If teachers are learners, what does that imply about the method by which they necessarily approach their work?

Principle 2: Reflection and inquiry are the methods by which teachers learn. These processes engage teachers in examining their practice and constructing new knowledge that will guide their future work.

Programs of professional development for teacher leadership need to teach teachers about the techniques of reflection and inquiry— what they are, why they are important, how to do them. These programs must also provide ample opportunity for guided practice whereby teachers can gain and embrace a reflective approach to their work in schools. Two factors of importance here are time and opportunity: Teachers need time and opportunity to learn to reflect and then time and opportunity to actually reflect on their work once they know how to do so.

If teachers learn through a process of reflective inquiry, what is it that they reflect about?

Principle 3: Teachers reflect about their past, present, and future experiences in school. Learning to view experience as the content of teacher reflection is an important part of professional development.

Although teachers learn from experience, they do not learn from it simply by having it; rather, they learn from experience when they have the time and capability to reflect on it. At all stages of their careers, teachers need to think about what they are doing, what they have done, and what they intend to do. Why they function as they do in practice is also part of the learning examination suggested by a constructivist view of reflective inquiry. Teachers need time set aside from their work with children and other classroom responsibilities to work with other school adults on matters of planning, curriculum development, problem solving, and assessment. The planned-for and enacted work of school experience constitutes the focus of teacher reflection, which suggests that professional education need not occur independently of teachers' real work but, rather, is connected to it in authentic ways.

If the focus of teacher reflection is experience, and if experience in schools is changing, complex, and fleeting, how can teachers be assisted in this process of reflecting on their work?

Principle 4: When teachers reflect, they reflect about something. Because this something is the "matters of school life," these matters or experiences of teachers must be captured in some form so that teachers can reflect about them.

The issue of "capturing" the matters of school life in a form that can be used to focus teacher reflection is an important one for professional development. Part of the professional development challenge is to create a "text" around which teacher reflection can occur. The criterion for this text is that it capture the authentic matters of school life. An articulated problem of practice might serve as such a text, as might a curriculum plan that needs to be negotiated, a videotape of children studying mathematics, and so forth. It is interesting to note that the creation of a text drawn from authentic practice creates at the same time an opportunity for teachers to step back from the demands of the practice that the text describes. This creation of space or distance situates the teacher learner apart from the experience itself and thus offers the opportunity for examining that practice in order to construct new knowledge about it. Stepping back from one's everyday experience to examine it, learn from it, place it in its larger context offers great potential for teacher learning that both responds to change and possibly directs it.

If teacher learning occurs when teachers reflect about their practices, and we know from constructivist learning theory that learning occurs best in relationship, how, then, do we bring relationship into the learning context for teaching?

> *Principle 5:* Not only do teachers need time and opportunity to reflect on their work, they need that time and opportunity to do so in the company of others with whom they can construct meaning.

This principle sets the stage for the collaborative learning context that we have argued strongly for throughout this book. Knowledge is socially constructed when people come together to make sense out of some part of the world they share in common. Creating opportunities for teachers to come together into a structure of collaborative conversation is a professional development strategy for both university-based and school-based teacher learning.

How do teachers construct meaning in these collaborative, reflective conversations about practice?

> *Principle 6:* To construct meaning (or to learn) within a collaborative context, teachers need the opportunity to speak and be heard as well as to listen and respond to the thoughts and beliefs of others.

Part of the power for learning of collaborative inquiry comes as people try to explain what they know and believe to others. As they do so, their collaborative colleagues respond with questions, comments, uncertainties, and support. The consequence of this exchange is the collective construction of new knowledge that is held in different forms by everyone present. By careful listening and thoughtful response, teachers help one another learn. In so doing, they themselves also learn, as does the organization of which they are a part.

Peter Senge, who has written extensively about organizational change, employs a learning metaphor to describe the way he sees organizations change. In a recent interview, he said, "a learning organization is one in which people at all levels are collectively and continually enhancing their capacity to create things they really want to create" (in O'Neil, 1995, p. 20). As teachers examine what they and their colleagues do in light of what they know and believe, and as they work to make sense of their world so they can act consciously toward the goals that they want to achieve, they are learning in the way Senge suggests. Teachers who participate in this thoughtful, wholehearted, and responsible inquiry that helps them and their colleagues learn are providing leadership of the sort we are conceptualizing in this text.

Who should be part of these collaborative conversations? Is there a guideline for establishing membership in the collaborative learning group?

> *Principle 7:* Collaborative learning groups in teaching should be structured to incorporate multiple perspectives because difference will stretch the opportunity to learn and better reflect the complex world of difference at the same time.

We have established that learning occurs more powerfully in social than in solitary settings and that therefore collaboration is critical to the learning process. It makes sense that with whom the collaboration occurs is also important. The membership of collaborative groups ought to vary according to the problem at hand; for different problems or issues, different people will need to be present. In general, collaborative groups should be composed of people concerned with the issue under discussion who have gathered because of their interest in and knowledge of the subject. Rather than organized along traditional lines (all third-grade teachers, all mathematics teachers, all preservice or all veteran teachers, etc.), the groups for this type of learning can be issue-based and multiperspective. Broadening the community builds ownership while combining the values of learning and caring. Also, as different teachers meet in different groupings to solve different problems, new alliances form, and a stronger network of interdependence arises.

If people with different points of view are brought together into these collaborative conversations, can we expect conflict to emerge? Does conflict inhibit learning?

> *Principle 8:* Conflict is a necessary outcome of a collaborative structure in which teachers come together to discuss issues of importance to them. Rather than inhibit learning, conflict can enhance it by causing people to stretch in their understandings and create alliances across differences that ultimately benefit everyone.

As was discussed in Chapter 6, we can expect conflict to arise as teachers work and learn in collaborative groups. Rather than attempting to avoid conflict, which has been the unsuccessful modus operandi for adults who work in school settings, our effort needs to be directed to learning to deal with it. Within the collaborative learning structure, opportunities need to be provided for people to learn how to anticipate conflict and plan for it, how to negotiate and resolve it, how to use it to enhance understanding, and so forth. Under the umbrella of learning conflict management, teachers can also learn more general collaboration skills, such as how to communicate effectively and enhance the communication capabilities of others, how to contribute to keeping a group's effort moving forward rather than stalling, how to generate and sustain external support, and so forth.

Do these skills of conflict negotiation, communication, and collaboration constitute leadership skills? Who should lead these collaborative groups, and how does leadership emerge?

> *Principle 9:* Given that they focus on different "matters at hand," collaborative learning groups need to accommodate changing leadership configurations according to the problem under consideration, the group's current membership, and what outcomes are needed.

In the conceptualization of constructivist teacher leadership that we are positing in this text, learning and leading are intimately connected; and each depends on the other. Leading, in fact, is defined in relationship to learning. Given the interrelationship of leading and learning as we have defined them here, we can expect that they will occur simultaneously within the context of a collaborative experience. Professional development must thus be structured to enhance both at the same time. Learning leadership skills can happen in the practice of collaborative work among school adults as teachers try their hands at leadership and are helped in reflecting about what worked and what did not. We have defined leadership as creating the occasion for others to learn. Given people's knowledge and skill, leadership can be consciously shared, with the more experienced leaders helping those less familiar with that responsibility. There need to be multiple opportunities for everyone to try moving the group through the process of learning together. Leadership can occur in many forms—it is important that everyone learn to see his or her opportunities for leadership and that each person be given the opportunity to learn to take the role of leader when the time is appropriate for him or her to do so.

Examples From Practice

In Chapter 4, we discussed the idea of learning communities and provided several examples with which we have had experience. By definition, learning communities foster learning in the people who are part of them. As such, learning communities can function to support the professional development of constructivist teacher leaders, and most that function as communities in this way do exactly that. By structure, the learning communities we discussed in Chapter 4 conform to the principles of teacher learning, leadership, and collaboration that we have outlined in the section above. For example, each involves teachers and other school adults working in collaborative settings to discuss matters of school practice, to construct meaning and define or redefine purpose. Each draws teachers and other adults together into conversations for problem solving, program planning, curriculum planning, teacher research, and so forth. These multiperspective conversations involve listening, speaking, negotiating, thinking, changing, learning, and leading. Given their structure and function, therefore, learning communities not only support the professional development of teacher leaders, but they also support and sustain school reform at the same time.

Let us take the example of a specific learning community presented in Chapter 4, the Teacher Action Research Project, and analyze it as to its congruence with the principles of professional development we have outlined in this chapter. A similar procedure might be useful for examining other learning communities to see if they provide a professional development opportunity that would support teacher learning for constructivist leadership. We will conclude by similarly analyzing a preservice teacher education program designed to address those principles as well. Our review of these programs is included to illustrate the approach we are taking to professional development, rather than to suggest these particular forms for other circumstances. The analysis of these two examples is meant to provoke a similar kind of thinking among people working toward the goal of preparing teachers to become constructivist leaders in schools.

The Teacher Action Research Project

The Teacher Action Research Project is part of a state-sponsored program designed to support school reform in California. It is a partnership program organized by the Bay Region IV Staff Development Consortium and includes the Consortium, a group of elementary, middle, and secondary schools involved in school reform, and a university department of education. The network of teacher researchers has grown to researchers investigating school change at upward of 30 or more Bay Area schools. From its inception in 1991, the Teacher Action Research Project has had as its primary goal supporting school reform by engaging teachers and administrators in a careful examination of the change process at their sites.

Reflection and inquiry combine to form the centerpiece of the Teacher Action Research Project, which addresses another of the principles of professional development described above. The full-day meetings of the research group are organized to help the researchers learn inquiry skills and practice them with a team of colleagues. In the context of this work, the teachers and administrators are asked to raise questions that cover a range of issues: the everyday practice of schooling, the change process at their sites, the process of school reform in general, or anything else that captures their attention or interest and relates to the group's focus on school change. As teachers work together to frame and reframe questions, they learn the value of questions for uncovering the uncertainty and complexity of life in schools. They also learn the value of working with others to frame better questions that ultimately focus more powerful learning.

In addition to learning about asking questions, the teacher researchers learn how to search for answers, a skill that is also critical to the processes of constructivist leadership. In the Teacher Action Research Project, teachers learn how to gather data, how to determine which data will be most useful for answering different questions, and how to analyze them once they are collected. These strategies are useful for constructivist leaders who collaborate with their colleagues in search of meaning and purpose for their work. Because these processes (asking questions, determining data-gathering-strategies, analyzing data) are all done in partnership or in teams, the teacher researchers have the opportunity to experience how knowledge is socially constructed through meaningful collaborative conversations among colleagues.

The teacher researchers also experience the challenge of dealing with conflicts that are inevitable in the context of these meaningful conversations. There are many times when the researchers talk through matters about which they hold strong beliefs, have firm convictions, or feel deeply. For example, the purpose of school is a frequent topic of importance in the conversation of teacher researchers. The purpose and direction of change is another. The value of reading for young children and the mechanism by which children learn to read are others, as are the value of collaboration for teachers as well as the mechanisms by which teachers learn that skill. Conflicts often surface when teachers have these conversations about important matters, and these conflicts need to be negotiated if the work of the teacher research group is to proceed.

Within the research process itself, there are several strategic points at which conflict can be expected and at which the collaborative process supports the researchers in learning to manage them. Choosing the research question with a partner is one example; reporting preliminary results at the site is another. Conflicts often arise when conversations are initiated about school change; therefore, the skills of negotiation, which are vital to constructivist leadership, are important to the teacher researcher as well. Teacher researchers can develop these skills while learning about the issues that the conflicts raise and about the process of moving through conflict to greater understanding.

Part of negotiating conflict is understanding it. By definition, the teacher researchers are working to understand school change in all of its infinite complexity. Their quest requires that they examine multiple points of view on matters of school life and the conflicts that those various points of view reveal. The process requires that they listen carefully to what their colleagues say to come to understand what they mean. According to many of the teacher researchers, listening carefully to their colleagues to understand them—and make sense of what they see and hear—may be the most powerful part of the learning they accomplish in their researcher role.

We argued earlier that when teachers reflect, they reflect about something. Capturing the "something" of school life is an important part of planning for collaborative work among teachers. It is also important to teacher learning, and teacher leading as well. Capturing the matters of school life to examine them carefully is a process built into the Teacher Action Research Project by both definition and design. The data that the researchers gather in all of its many forms (surveys, documents already on hand at the school, interviews that are recorded and transcribed, minutes from restructuring meetings, etc.) create a "text," which is subsequently used to focus the teacher researcher conversations about practice and change. In addition, the researchers themselves create their own text in the form of stories or other documents that they write in an early stage of the process (Richert, 1995).

As the various texts about school change are created, the researchers organize and present them for review and examination in both site-based and cross-site meetings. Again, these collaborative meetings, which are typically focused by some part of the research text, are attended by various constituencies involved in various parts of the school change process. In the research group itself, there is ample conversation about the data that different groups bring to the meetings, the stories particular researchers tell and write, the formulations and findings of the researchers during the process, and so forth. Additionally, collaborative conversations that occur outside of the research group still use the research texts as a focus. Often the text will create conflict as well as conversation as the group examining it works together to construct meaning from what they see, read, and hear. Given the role of creator of the text, or historian of the change process, or researcher of the process, the teacher researcher is called on to lead these conversations as well as the activities that follow from them. Learning to lead, then, is an important outcome of the process as well.

Teachers for Tomorrow's Schools: A Case Example of Preservice Teacher Education

The position we have taken about learning to lead in a constructivist way in the context of school rests on an assumption about learning in teaching that must be established early in a teacher's career and fostered throughout. Preservice teacher education plays a critical role in setting the stage for a learning approach to teaching; it provides the foundation on which constructivist teacher leadership is based. Novices must develop a sense of their role as teacher that allows them to depart from traditional images of teaching and school and to replace them with images of what teaching and schooling might become. To accomplish this, novice teachers need to have the opportunity to surface their beliefs so that they can acknowledge and examine them. Similarly, they must have the opportunity to cast as "problematic" rather than "given" the realities of school as they inherit it—realities such as the hierarchical organization of school leadership, the isolation of teachers from one another and from other adults, the schedule of bells that fragments the day into arbitrary bits, the separation of subject matters that suggests that mathematics does not require knowing English and biology has nothing to do with art, the organization of children into groupings by age, the division of children by "ability," and so forth. Again, they must have the opportunity to examine those factors as they are and to imagine how they might be if schools were better able to respond not only to change but also to the people whom they are designed to serve.

Given the principles of professional development we discussed earlier in this chapter, how might a teacher education program at the preservice level be designed to launch the career of a constructivist teacher leader? How might we prepare a teacher who is able to critically examine the norms and realities of practice as we know it and create occasions for both children and adults to more powerfully learn in the institution of school? What might such a program look like? The Teachers for Tomorrow's Schools (TTS) program at Mills College in California is structured to prepare novice teachers with the knowledge, skills, and commitments of the constructivist teacher leader and promote the type of professional learning and leading we have argued for in this text. Let us examine some of the structures and processes of the Mills TTS program to determine how the principles of professional development for constructivist teacher leadership might guide the practice of preservice teacher education. Again, this brief analysis is meant to serve as an example of how the faculty at one college have constructed their program to address the purposes they have set for themselves and to meet the needs of their students and broader community. Other institutions with different purposes and constituencies would undoubtedly approach their work in a different way.

Like the work of the learning communities described in Chapter 4 and the work of the Teacher Action Research Project described earlier in this chapter, the TTS program at Mills couples reflection and constructivism as it conceptualizes the task of preparing teachers to meet the challenge of change in schools. The name Teachers for Tomorrow's Schools implies a forward-looking conception of both teaching and school. Given the inevitability of change, the Mills program focuses the work of learning to teach on the process of examining both what *is* in schools as we know them and what *ought to be* as well. The method of inquiry that Mills teachers learn to employ is characterized by the tenets of reflective practice: Teachers learn to ask questions of the world they see and experience to understand it and then act in it. In this approach, reflection leads to action, which leads to further reflection, and so on. Given that the world they view is not only infinitely complex but changing as well, the Mills teachers learn to conduct this reflective examination in collaboration with others who can help them see the world more fully, more clearly, and more accurately. As they construct their questions and begin to search for answers in collaboration with others, therefore, Mills teachers come to recognize their role in fostering the learning of their colleagues as well as themselves. They learn to challenge one another to look harder and farther and not to accept as given those things about school that appear to be true. They learn to respond to the provocations of others in turn. As they listen, learn, and create the conditions by which others do the same, they also learn to lead. The question now is how is this done? How is the program organized and conducted to accomplish these goals?

Program structure, content, and process all contribute to creating a teacher education learning community at Mills that initiates novice teachers into their constructivist leadership roles. Given the belief that knowledge is socially constructed, the program structures most of the learning opportunities as collaborative experiences in which students and faculty work together to examine the workings of school. These groups of colleagues study school practice to learn from it, make sense of it, and construct new knowledge about it as well. The groups that are created at Mills occur along both traditional and nontraditional lines. To begin, Teachers for Tomorrow's Schools is a kindergarten through 12th-grade program designed to bring elementary and secondary teachers into substantive contact with one another. Though the student teachers choose a specialty area that will focus part of their academic work, there are numerous events and activities in which they work with one another across grade levels and subject areas. Given the program goal of unifying rather than fragmenting teachers and their work, teachers are positioned as having more in common with their colleagues in other subjects and in other grade levels than they have differences. In addition to having their subject matter or grade-level cohorts, the students are also placed in a second cohort that is mixed in its composition.

To establish a sense of community built on norms of collegiality, the program has only one entry point each year. All students begin in the fall and end at the end of the public school year in June. Much of the work of the program is done in collaborative groups with different students or faculty participating as leaders. A community is built as student teachers work together and with their faculty to confront the uncertainty of school and examine the dilemmas of practice. "The work of school is too complex and too changing for teachers to do it alone," the student teachers are told many times. "We are in this together—we need one another to meet the challenge of making school work better for a greater percentage of the children and adults they are meant to serve." In the context of these collaborative conversations, relationships are formed and alliances created; thus, a norm of collegiality becomes institutionalized as the credential year progresses.

Though the academic course work at Mills is organized in fairly traditional ways with regard to courses offered and content covered, the methodology of the courses and their internal organization reflects a changing conception of what it means to teach and what novice teachers need to know. Students conduct much of the work of the courses in collaboration with their peers who are sometimes in the same subject area or grade level and sometimes not. Depending on background knowledge and expertise, the students assume various leadership roles, which they come to see as part of their responsibility to their colleagues, their students, and themselves. The student teacher who assumes leadership for a cross-grade-level ecoliteracy curriculum project on cycles, for example, may assume a different role when the group meets again to discuss the issue of grades. Leadership for the various tasks shifts, and the tasks themselves change over the course of the year.

Interestingly, reflection and inquiry frame both the content emphasis of the Mills program and the pedagogy as well. The novice teachers learn to take an inquiring stance toward their work, and they learn to do the work of reflective practice at the same time. Given the stage in the teacher's career, there is considerable content to learn regarding children, learning, schooling, subject matter pedagogy, and so forth. However, all of this content is presented through a problem-solving and inquiry methodology whereby the novice teachers ask questions of the practice they experience in their fieldwork and search for answers based on the theoretical perspectives they are coming to know or the theoretical positions they are beginning to construct. Theory has a stronghold in the Mills program as a foundation on which teachers can construct meaningful questions of practice and against which they can challenge the practice they see and do. "Theory and practice are part of the same continuum," they are told by faculty who draw on the teachings of Dewey. "Each informs and challenges the other, and as the process proceeds, more powerful theories emerge."

Various methodologies that teach the norms of collaborative inquiry as well as the skills of reflection are commonplace in the Mills program. Case methods in which the student teachers write their own cases of practice and then present them to a group of their colleagues are used to examine issues of diversity, subject matter teaching, and the ethical dimensions of the workings of school. Portfolios and video cases are used to help the student teachers inquire into matters of practice that lead to defining one's professional self. The exercise proceeds with presenting that professional self to others. Action research frames several program experiences in which the student teachers work with others to understand a problem of practice, design a plan to address it, and then evaluate that plan in preparation for further work.

The Mills program is structured by a shared perspective among the faculty: They believe that schools are not as they ought to be and that schools can become different. The teacher education agenda, then, becomes twofold. On the one hand, student teachers need to learn the knowledge and skills that will allow them to be successful in schools as they are. At the same time, they need to develop the commitment, as well as the knowledge and skill, to help them work effectively to create schools that better meet the needs of the people they serve. The knowledge, skills, and commitments of constructivist leadership need to be established early in a teacher's career and fostered throughout. In preservice teacher education, the foundation for constructivist leadership can be laid. By embracing uncertainty, teaching the skills of reflective practice, instilling the norm of collegiality, expecting a rigorous examination of the workings of school, and providing the space and challenge to dream, the Mills program attempts to lay the foundation for its graduates to do this very important work.

Concluding Thoughts

This chapter has presented a conception of teacher development that links teacher learning and school change. If we believe that schools need to change in some significant ways and if we believe that teachers are best situated to guide this agenda of change, then we need to extend our consideration of change to the preparation of the teachers we hope will do this work. Interestingly, the preparation of teachers for the work of constructivist leadership cannot, by definition, be conceived of as a one-shot or two-shot (preservice/ inservice) enterprise. Rather, the ongoing learning of teachers and the learning of the schools in which they work might be seen as the driving force of the change agenda itself. Teachers who come together in pursuit of a dream must lead one another to learn and grow and change. As they strengthen their ability to learn together and do this collaborative work, the institutions that house them will necessarily also change. Perhaps the biggest challenge to professional development, and consequently the biggest challenge to the promise of change itself, is to instill images of the possible in the minds and hope in the hearts of the teachers who lead. To instill those images and that hope, we must construct them for ourselves as well. We must also (and at the same time) work to create the conditions in schools that someday will allow those images to become real.

The Future of Teaching, Leading, and Reform

The Web

This we know.
The earth does not belong to us;
we belong to the earth.
This we know.
All things are connected
like the blood which unites one family.
Whatever befalls the earth
befalls the sons and the daughters of the earth.
We did not weave the web of life;
we are merely a strand in it.
Whatever we do to the web,
we do to ourselves.

Attributed to Chief Seattle

The six young Latino men shuffled their feet on the wooden floor. Ill-fitting clothes, somewhat outdated, revealed a shared lack of attention to such amenities. Their eyes moved uneasily across the room. A few feet away, several women and a few men appeared equally uncomfortable. This was not the usual opening of events in this venerable classroom.

The staff development consortium facilitator had arranged for these six young prisoner gang members to talk with the group about their experiences in school.

The facilitator welcomed the group, describing the purpose of this dialogue. The men relaxed somewhat. "Can you tell us about what school was like for you?" queried the facilitator. Silence encompassed the room, pushing hard at the old walls.

Finally one began, "It wasn't bad until after sixth grade—then nobody cared about me anymore." The others nodded.

One of the teacher participants asked, "What do you mean?"

"Well," started another, "in grade school my teacher would get after me when I did something wrong. If I cut school, she would call Mom. When I wasn't working, she would come over to me and say, 'Hey, Carlos'—she would always say 'Hey Carlos'—'get yourself working or you're never going to be anything!'"

"Yeah," said another, "my teacher was sorta like that—she'd talk to me, you know, like she thought I might amount to something."

"And then what happened?"

Another man offered, "When I got to junior high, no one talked to you—just suspend you or put you in detention."
"That's when I got in with the Clips—a bunch of guys—we'd hang around, talk about stuff, when I couldn't figure stuff out, we'd talk about it."

"I joined the Reds," said another. "Same kind of thing. You know, at first it was just a bunch of guys to talk with."

"We started to get into trouble, one guy would bring some drugs, we'd lift some things from the stores. Then we got into the heavy-duty things, filling stations at first."

"When I was in high school, I got suspended. And when I went back, the principal told me I could only take this one voc class—but I told him, 'I want to learn to read, man. I want to learn to read!' No one ever heard me."

The stories unfolded through the evening, stories of loneliness, rage, sorrow, and hopelessness.

Dramas like this true story are being lived all over the United States—stories of separation, loss, and longing for community. In gangs, each of these young men—now serving 7 to 12 years for robbery and assault—found companionship, ready listeners, people who cared about them. They formed loyalties that overrode fragile judgment, that superseded fledging values. What they could not find were adults and other children who could bring a sense of values and purpose to their lives that could set a different kind of direction and create a sense of possible future.

The reform agenda is about our children and their possible futures. It is about the need for resiliency, caring, meaningful service, developing competence, and planning for the future. It is about community. We know how to provide this quality of life in schools, yet we seldom do so.

In a 1995 Office of Education Research and Improvement (OERI) study, Rossi and Stringfield (1995) explain,

> By the year 2020, the majority of students in America's public schools will be living in circumstances traditionally regarded as placing them at risk of educational failure. Many will be poorly housed, undernourished, subject to the effects of others' abuse of drugs, and provided with few positive adult role models. A greater number of young people will be neglected or abused by those adults who enter their lives and— because of misunderstandings, insufficient resources, or a lack of regard for individual differences and capabilities— *treated harshly by the very institutions that ostensibly were created to help them.*

Seymour Sarason (1995), a veteran observer of the American scene, comments,

> I agree with Rossi and Stringfield. And if they are right . . . then by 2020 public dissatisfaction with our schools will have brought a partial dismantling of the public school system. The danger to society is that whatever drastic changes will have been effected will have been undertaken out of desperation, not inspiration.

In the spring of 1996, a poll released by Policy Analysis for California Education, or PACE, reported that only 5% of Californians believe that the state's public schools offer a quality education (Tuller, 1996). Just as Sarason predicted, the same poll identified some of the "desperate" measures that respondents were inclined to support to deal with the perceived crisis: competency tests for teachers, standardized tests to measure student achievement, and automatic expulsion of students who bring drugs or guns or other weapons to schools. Fear is sure to evoke such responses—responses that evidence little connection to caring communities, professional judgment, and systemic change.

In Chapter 1, we suggested several context issues that are contributing to a desperate response. Throughout this book, we have challenged educators to alter the contexts in which we find ourselves—to lead through inspiration.

Yet a glaring question is raising its troublesome head: Can the same people who have created today's schools lead the reform of these same schools? Can educators who have depersonalized the learning lives of the six young men above—and millions like them—create the new schools of tomorrow?

Who Is Responsible for Reform?

The dilemmas and problems facing our schools, as well as the solutions, are systemic—that is, context issues create conditions that re-create behaviors and new context. It is a dynamic process in which everyone has a stake and a responsibility. Blame is a moot point, for there is no one group or person to blame. We are all responsible.

Throughout this book, we have suggested that teachers are particularly well situated to lead the reform agenda. We stand by that assertion. However, we are not so naive as to believe that even teachers with new skills, good will, and passionate intentions can affect major reforms without significant changes in the policies and structures that govern our educational systems.

Changing system norms for the next century requires new ways of thinking and behaving that entail a shift in policies and structures that reinforce the current context of education in the United States.

Policy Reform Recommendations to Support Emerging Teacher Leadership

The following recommendations will frame our new assumptions about teacher knowledge and evaluation, power relationships in districts, structures that support community, and administrative succession. Many of these recommendations will require legislative action; a few can be accomplished through changes in perspectives. They are not intended to be prescriptive but to open the dialogue around issues of vital importance to schooling.

Teacher Preparation and Credentialing

We have consistently noticed that teachers who have advanced opportunities for learning, usually (but not always) beyond their own schools and districts, develop a maturity, consciousness, and identity that are strikingly different from teachers who do not have such experiences. These advanced opportunities may be graduate degree programs in universities, action research consortia, professional networks, or administrative preparation programs. Currently, professional development schools, which operate in the home districts, may be an exception to this rule, and the apparent growth observed in teachers involved with them may stem from their work with university faculty within the school context. Restructuring schools may represent an additional exceptional local setting; often individuals in such settings are part of a larger professional network.

The development of the commitments, knowledge, and skills that are needed by teacher leaders requires such an advanced professional experience. We recommend the establishment of a Professional Leadership Development Preparation Tier for teachers: a second level of preparation that would not begin until after the fifth year of teaching. This program would emphasize knowledge generation and inquiry; reflection, dialogue, and writing; advanced curriculum and assessment development; leadership and the development of reform agenda. These programs would provide teachers and other leaders with experiences of being in mature learning communities so they could develop images and forms to take back to their own settings. Partnerships and "critical friendships" with others in professional communities outside the school setting would be established so that these relationships would be ongoing—part of the process for keeping schools directly connected to the larger professional community. Our intention is that such a credentialing requirement could "sunset" after a decade—about the length it would take to establish substantive learning communities in schools.

Unlike most credential programs, we would suggest that these requirements be met through the provision of options, choices in format, setting, and focus. Numerous options could be identified, depending on the availability of advanced learning opportunities in various regions of the United States.

This shift in teacher preparation would allow for administrative preparation programs to be more limited in scope. In California, for instance, the Professional Administrative Services Credential (second tier) could be eliminated in favor of the more extensive preparation at the professional level of teaching. Administrative certificate programs could focus on administrative skills, such as law, finance, policy, and community relations, needed by teachers who had completed the Advanced Professional Preparation Program for teachers.

Principal Succession

With Advanced Professional Preparation and availability of the additional administrative certificate, teachers in a school could more easily succeed principals. Schools could be led by leadership teams of teachers, with perhaps one person designated as principal teacher. This practice would mean that the learning community would be continually preparing its future "principals." The likelihood of keeping sustained focus on a coherent reform agenda and on relationships would be greatly enhanced. The loss of continuity when schools lose their principals is dramatic; teacher succession would address this issue.

We recognize, however, that there is nothing sacred in teachers becoming the next principals of their own schools. We have seen too many circumstances in which teachers can be just as autocratic as some administrators. Without advanced preparation for teachers, we would not make this accompanying recommendation on succession.

Teacher Evaluation

The current practice of creating a controlling, top-down evaluation system to supposedly protect the district from the estimated 5% of teachers who perform poorly is antiquated and indefensible. This 5% rule has been the norm in districts across the land; it results in an evaluation system that gravely inhibits the growth of all teachers (while not succeeding with the 5%).

It was heartening to read Tom McGreal's description of the state of evaluation in the United States (Brandt, 1996). McGreal's work on teacher evaluation emphasizes professional growth and team learning rather than evaluation. He reports that "probably 150 school districts are into this actively, that as many as a thousand others could be moving in this direction.... When school boards understand what we're trying to do, they accept it. . . . We'll guarantee accountability, but don't make us build an evaluation system for one or two bad eggs" (p. 32).

Teachers, like everyone else, learn from continual feedback. The aim is to develop an inquiring, learning cycle that provides continual feedback to everyone in the learning community. This means that when teachers involve themselves in learning opportunities such as portfolio assessment, action research, team or peer coaching, working in leadership teams, or collaborative planning, they are being evaluated all the time. Professional development and evaluation become one and the same. Such a comprehensive view of professional development can lead to self-responsibility and shared school accountability.

Finding Time to Learn

As we have noted, collaborative learning time is essential to the building of a learning community. This is fairly common knowledge—yet it is not commonly acted on, primarily because it has meant taking time away from children. Policymakers, members of the business community, and many parents have been particularly unsympathetic to this issue.

Finding time for everyone to learn is going to mean extending the length of the school year so that professional time can become a regular part of schooling. In addition, it is going to mean paying teachers more for that longer year. But working with an antiquated, nine-month school year (minus holidays) will not allow everyone in the school community to learn adequately.

In the meantime, states, districts, and communities must support collaborative time in schools or the complex problems of schooling are never going to be tackled with the vigor and depth that are needed.

Teachers Associations

We have noted at several points in this book our concern about the local stances taken by associations (unions). These issues vary tremendously among the states, even among states with a heavy union influence. For instance, unions in New York and Michigan are supporting small schools, professional time, and alternative evaluation measures, whereas in California, local unions often oppose restructuring efforts and support incompetent teachers.

Clearly, these variations on the same themes are not coming from the national level, where professional development and school improvement are important agendas. In many ways, the local union affiliates become as embedded in mechanistic, bureaucratic thinking and practices as other institutions within the system. It will therefore be up to the teachers at the local levels to shape association policy in regard to support of professional time, teacher peer assessment and support of poorly performing teachers, support for new teachers, and shared governance.

A "New Federalism": The District and the School

Several experiments are underway within school districts that might be characterized as *federalism*—defined by the *American Heritage Dictionary* (Soukhanov & Severynse, 1992) as "a system of government in which power is divided between a central authority and constituent political units." In several states, charter schools have been established to divide and delegate powers to the schools. In Chicago and New York, "minidistricts" were created that replicated the larger school district, complete with local school board.

Our interest here is in sharing power that would begin to dismantle the hierarchy and establish more of a coherent network of interdependent units (schools, district, programs). Clearly, setting up competitive political units (additional school boards) does not have that effect. The Chicago and New York initiatives have demonstrated both the power of decentralization and the danger that making political units smaller is not enough, that the quality and character of the power that is to be shared must also change.

We would propose sharing power by sharing responsibilities for specific functions, strategies, and tasks needed within a congruent value framework. For instance,

What if all schools were viewed as semiautonomous but inter-dependent units that develop collaborative compacts with their district offices, reciprocal agreements that specify the services, functions, and responsibilities that will be performed at each level (school and district)?

What if the major authority and responsibility for most instructional areas, such as professional development, shifted to the local school level but with several caveats?

- Responsibility for systematic accountability came with authority for functions
- Coherent systemwide standards (collaboratively developed by the district and schools) would be central to the professional accountability system
- The community (local school and the broader district) would be informed and engaged in the development of standards

What if the accountability system (at both school and district level) were of the professional kind advocated earlier in the chapter—one focused on systematic inquiry around evidence concerning both student and adult work?

What if schools and the district were all continuously striving to become self-organizing interdependent learning communities of the kind that this book envisions?

What if one of the functions of a restructured school board were to be the adjudication of what rights and responsibilities fall at the school level and which are districtwide?

Sharing power within a district to begin to move the hierarchy to a network is one of the more difficult policy changes that confronts us. It will take imaginative and talented board members, superintendents, principals, and teachers—all working together—to begin this experiment. Initially, we would expect to see a few pioneer districts working through alternative ways of accomplishing this goal.

A Vision of the New Road Ahead

We envision that this network of dense relationships that form a learning community will be led primarily by teachers working with administrators, students, parents, and the broader communities. Leading—like learning—will be seen as everyone's work. We will come to understand that learning occurs as we construct meaning and knowledge together in a caring community. Each of these communities—learning, school, and caring—will be understood as moral communities that exist for the growth and development of its inhabitants.

Teachers as constructivist leaders will envision and facilitate the learning in these communities as they

- perceive themselves as powerful professional colleagues;
- cocreate community for all members of the broader community;
- engage others in the work of leadership;
- work with principals and others to redefine roles and responsibilities;
- create meaning and knowledge with others, including members of the broader community such as district personnel, professional organizations and networks, and university faculty;
- actively solicit critical feedback and honestly generate and share information and use it to make wise decisions leading to action;
- exercise authority in relation to the district, unions, and other organizations and agencies;
- create opportunities for learning in many settings; and
- learn from, and enable the learning of, students.

This time, the reform agenda must be led by those who are closest to the classroom and to the parents, by those who can commit to a community, and by those who have the knowledge and understandings of teaching and learning. Teachers can save our schools—if only they believe it to be so.

References

Anderman, E. M., & Maehr, M. L. (1994). Motivation and schooling in the middle grades. *Review of Educational Research, 62*(2), 287-309.

Bailey, S. (1995a). Structured dialogue: Inserting new cultural norms one conversation at a time. *ASCD presents: Satellite broadcasts with Suzanne Bailey—Part II*. Alexandria, VA: Association for Supervision and Curriculum Development.

Bailey, S. (1995b, March). *Systems change: Detecting and intervening in strong organizational patterns, preferences and habits*. Paper presented at the annual conference of the Association for Supervision and Curriculum Development, San Francisco, CA.

Ball, S. J. (1987). *The micropolitics of the school: Toward a theory of school organization*. London: Methuen.

Barth, R. (1988). School: A community of leaders. In A. Lieberman (Ed.), *Building successful cultures in schools* (pp. 129-147). New York: Teachers College Press.

Bateson, G. (1972). *Steps to an ecology of mind*. San Francisco: Ballantine.

Bateson, M. C. (1994). *Peripheral visions*. New York: HarperCollins.

Battistich, V., Solomon, D., Kim, D., Watson, M., & Schaps, E. (1995). Schools as communities, poverty levels of student populations, and students' attitudes, motives, and performance: A multilevel analysis. *American Educational Research Journal, 32*(3), 627-658.

Bell, C., & Chase, S. (1993). The underrepresentation of women in school leadership. In C. Marshall & P. Zodhiates (Eds.), *The new politics of race and gender: The 1992 yearbook of the politics of education association* (pp. 141-154). Washington, DC: Falmer.

Bicklen, S. (1985). Can elementary school teaching be a career? A search for new ways of understanding women's needs. *Issues in Education, 3*(3), 215-231.

Blackford, S. (1995). *School improvement and a community of leaders.* Hayward: California State University, Hayward, Center for Educational Leadership.

Block, P. (1993). *Stewardship: Choosing service over self-interest.* San Francisco: Berrett-Koehler.

Bolman, L. G., & Deal, T. E. (1991). *Reframing organizations: Artistry, choice and leadership.* San Francisco: Jossey-Bass.

Brandt, R. (1996, March). On a new direction for teacher evaluation: A conversation with Tom McGreal. *Educational Leadership, 53*(6), 30-33.

Bridges, E. M. (1992). *Problem-based learning for administrators.* Eugene: University of Oregon. (ERIC Document Reproduction Service No. EA023722)

Brooks, M., & Grennon-Brooks, J. (1993). *In search of understanding: The case for constructivist classrooms.* Alexandria, VA: Association for Supervision and Curriculum Development.

Bruner, J. S. (1966). *Toward a theory of instruction.* New York: Norton.

Bruner, J., & Haste, H. (Eds.). (1987). *Making sense: The child's construction of the world.* New York: Methuen.

Bullough, R., Knowles, G., & Crow, N. (1991). *Emerging as a teacher.* London: Routledge.

Capra, F. (1995). From the parts to the whole: Systems thinking in ecology and education. *Professional Development Briefs 4,* 1-8. (Available from the Center for Ecoliteracy, 2522 San Pablo Blvd., Berkeley, CA 94702)

Capra, F. (in press). *The web of life.* London: HarperCollins.

Capra, F., & Steindl-Rast, D. (1991). *Belonging to the universe: Explorations on the frontiers of science and spirituality.* New York: HarperCollins.

Carter, S. (1989). Incentives and rewards to teaching. In D. Warren (Ed.), *American teachers: Histories of a profession at work* (pp. 49-62. New York: American Educational Research Association.

Cliff, R., Johnson, M., Holland, P., & Veal, M. (1992). Developing the potential for collaborative school leadership. *American Educational Research Journal, 29*(4), 877-908.

Cochran-Smith, M. (1991). Learning to teach against the grain. *Harvard Educational Review, 61*(3), 279-310.

Cohn, M., & Kottkamp, R. (1993). *Teachers: The missing voice in education.* Albany: SUNY Press.

Collay, M. (1988). *Dialogue as a language of learning: An ethnographic study of teacher socialization.* Unpublished doctoral dissertation, University of Oregon, Eugene.

Collay, M. (1996, February). *NBPTS and the portfolio: Teachers assess their practice.* Paper presented at the American Association of Colleges for Teacher Education, Chicago, IL.

Collay, M., & Gagnon, G. (1995, Summer). *Reflections on the profession of teaching.* Paper presented at the 7th Biennial Conference of the International Study Association on Teacher Thinking, St. Catharines, Ontario, Canada.

Comer, J. P. (1980). *School power.* New York: Macmillan.

Cuban, L. (1984). *How teachers taught.* New York: Longman.

Darling-Hammond, L. (1990). Teachers and teaching: Signs of a changing profession. In W. R. Houston (Ed.), *The handbook of research on teacher education* (pp. 267-290). New York: Macmillan.

Darling-Hammond, L. (1993). Reframing the school reform agenda: Developing the capacity for school transformation. *Phi Delta Kappan, 74*(10), 753-761.

Darling-Hammond, L. (1996). The quiet revolution: Rethinking teacher development. *Educational Leadership, 53*(6), 4-10.

Darling-Hammond, L., & McLaughlin, M. (1995). Policies that support professional development in an era of reform. *Phi Delta Kappan, 76*(8), 597-604.

Deming, E. W. (1982). *Out of crisis.* Cambridge, MA: MIT Press.

DeVries, R., & Kohlberg, L. (1987). *Programs of early education: The constructivist view.* White Plains, NY: Longman.

Dewey, J. (1916). *Democracy and education.* New York: Macmillan.

Dewey, J. (1933). *How we think.* Chicago: Regnery.

Dewey, J. (1938). *Experience and education.* New York: Macmillan.

Dietz, M. E. (1991). *Professional development portfolio: Facilitator's guide.* Shoreham, NY: Frameworks.

Dietz, M. E. (1993, July). *Professional development portfolio: A constructivist approach to teacher development.* Session conducted at the Annual Conference of Critical Thinking, Massachusetts Institute of Technology, Boston, MA.

Dietz, M. E. (1995). Using portfolio as a framework for professional development. *Journal of Staff Development, 16*(2), 40-43.

Distad, L. (1994). *The teacher at work: Finding it difficult to breathe.* Unpublished doctoral dissertation, University of St. Thomas, St. Paul, MN.

Duke, D. (1994). Drift, detachment, and the need for teacher leadership. In D. R. Walling (Ed.), *Teachers as leaders* (pp. 255-273). Bloomington, IN: Phi Delta Kappa.

Dunlap, D. M., & Goldman, P. (1991, February). Rethinking power in schools. *Educational Administration Quarterly, 27*(1), 5-29.

Dunlap, D. M., & Schmuck, P. A. (eds.) (1994). *Women leading in education.* Albany: SUNY Press.

Edmonds, R. (1979, October). Effective schools for the urban poor. *Educational Leadership, 37*(1), 15-24.

Flexner, S. B. (Ed.). (1987). *The Random House dictionary of the English language* (2nd ed., unabridged). New York: Random House.

Fraser, B. J. (1991). Two decades of classroom environment research. In B. J. Fraser & H. J. Walberg (Eds.), *Educational environments: Evaluation, antecedents and consequences* (pp. 3-27). Oxford, England: Pergamon.

Freire, P. (1970). *Pedagogy of the oppressed.* New York: Continuum.

Fullan, M. (1993). *Change forces: Probing the depths of educational reform.* Bristol, PA: Falmer.

Fullan, M. (1994). Teacher leadership: A failure to conceptualize. In D. R. Walling (Ed.), *Teachers as leaders* (pp. 241-253). Bloomington, IN: Phi Delta Kappa.

Fullan, M. (1995, December). *Navigating the winds of change.* Keynote address at the National Staff Development Council conference, Chicago.

Futrell, M. H. (1994). Empowering teachers as learners and leaders. In D. R. Walling (Ed.), *Teachers as leaders* (pp. 119-135). Bloomington, IN: Phi Delta Kappa.

Gardner, M., & Lambert, L. (1993, April). *Women's ways of leading.* Multimedia presentation given at California State University, Hayward, CA.

Gessert-Wigfield, A., & Vann Gardner, A. (in press). We've been framed—again: A case study of the relationship between reframing, school culture, and the change process. *Case studies of whole school change.* (Available from the Bay Region IV Professional Development Consortium, 101 Twin Dolphin Dr., Redwood City, CA 94065)

Gilligan, C. (1982). *In a different voice: Psychological theory of women's development.* Cambridge, MA: Harvard University Press.

Glickman, C. (1993). *Renewing America's schools: A guide for school-based action.* San Francisco: Jossey-Bass.

Goldstein, J. (1994). *The unshackled organization: Facing the challenge of unpredictability through spontaneous reorganization.* Portland, OR: Productivity Press.

Graves, S. (1995). *Merits of the professional development portfolio: A framework for continuous growth.* Unpublished doctoral dissertation, University of Dayton, OH.

Greene, M. (1988). *The dialectic of freedom.* New York: Teachers College Press.

Grossman, P. L., & Stodolsky, S. S. (1995). Content as context: The role of school subjects in secondary school teaching. *Educational Researcher, 24,* 5-11.

Grumet, M. (1980). *Bittermilk.* Amherst: University of Massachusetts Press.

Heifetz, R. A. (1994). *Leadership without easy answers.* Cambridge, MA: Belknap.

Herbst, J. (1989). *And sadly teach: Teacher education and professionalization in American culture.* Madison: University of Wisconsin Press.

Hock, D. W. (1995). Institutions in the age of mindcrafting. *Annals of Earth, 13*(2).

Holmes Group, Inc. (1990). *Tomorrow's schools: Principles for the design of Professional Development Schools.* East Lansing, MI: Author.

Hurty, K. S. (1995). Women principals—leading with power. In D. M. Dunlap & P. A. Schmuck, P. A. (Eds.), *Women leading in education* (pp. 380-406). Albany: State University of New York Press.

Jones, A. W. (1995). *The soul's journey.* San Francisco: Harper.

Kanter, R. M. (1983). *The change masters: Innovation and entrepreneurship in the American corporation.* New York: Simon & Schuster.

Kegan, R. (1982). *The evolving self: Problems and process in human development.* Cambridge, MA: Harvard University Press.

Kent, K. (1985). A successful program of teachers assisting teachers. *Educational Leadership, 43*(3), 30-33.

Kent, K., & Abbey, T. (1995). Collaborative work cultures, learning communities and school change. *Cooperative Learning, 15*(1), 21-25.

Kent, K., & Ellman, J. (1990, April). *Developmentalism goes to school: A teacher's first year experience.* Paper presented at the annual meeting of the American Educational Research Association, Boston.

Kent, K., & Gemmet, R. (1990-1995). [Project documentation, notes, reflections, and presentation materials]. Unpublished raw data.

Kohlberg, L. (1976). Moral stages and moralization: The cognitive developmental approach. In T. Lickona (Ed.), *Moral development and behavior* (pp. 31-53). New York: Holt, Rinehart & Winston.

Kozol, J. (1991). *Savage inequalities.* New York: Harper.

Krupp, A. (1995, December). *Award acceptance.* Presented at the annual meeting of National Staff Development Council, Chicago:

Laird, S. (1988). Reforming "Woman's true profession": A case for "feminist pedagogy" in teacher education? *Harvard Educational Review, 58*(4), 449-463.

Lambert, L. (1988). Staff development redesigned. *Phi Delta Kappan 69*(9), 665-668.

Lambert, L. (1989). The end of an era of staff development. *Educational Leadership 7*, 78-83.

Lambert, L., Walker, D., Zimmerman, D., Cooper, J., Lambert, M., Gardner, M., & Ford-Slack, P. J. (Eds.). (1995). *The constructivist leader.* New York: Teachers College Press.

Lambert, M., & Gardner, M. (1995). The school district as interdependent learning community. In L. Lambert, D. Walker, D. Zimmerman, J. Cooper, M. Gardner, & P. J. Ford-Slack (Eds.), *The constructivist leader* (pp. 134-158). New York: Teachers College Press.

Lieberman, A. (1995). Practices that support teacher development: Transforming conceptions of professional learning. *Phi Delta Kappan, 76*(8), 591-596.

Lieberman, A., & Miller, L. (1990). The social realities of teaching. In A. Lieberman (Ed.), *Schools as collaborative cultures: Creating the future now* (pp. 153-163). London: Falmer.

Lieberman, A., Saxl, E., & Miles, M. B. (1988). Teacher leadership: Ideology and practice. In A. Lieberman (Ed.), *Building a professional culture in schools.* New York: Teachers College Press.

Lipsitz, J. (1984). *Successful schools for young adolescents.* New Brunswick, NJ: Transaction.

Little, J. W. (1982). Norms of collegiality and experimentation: Workplace conditions of school success. *AERA Journal, 19*(3), 325-340.

Little, J. W. (1990). Teachers as colleagues. In A. Lieberman (Ed.), *Schools as collaborative cultures: Creating the future now* (pp. 165-193). London: Falmer.

Loevinger, J. (1976). *Ego development: Conceptions and theories.* San Francisco: Jossey-Bass.

Lortie, D. (1975). *Schoolteacher.* Chicago: University of Chicago Press.

Macy, J. (1994-95, Winter). Viewpoints. *Noetic Sciences Bulletin,* p. 2.

Malone, D. (1962). *Jefferson and the ordeal of liberty.* Boston: Little, Brown.

Marshall, S. P., & Hatcher, C. (1996). Promoting career development through CADRE. *Educational Leadership, 53*(6), 42-46.

Mattingly, P. (1975). *The classless profession: American schoolmen in the nineteenth century.* New York: New York University Press.

McClelland, D. C. (1945). *Power: The inner experience.* New York: Irvington.

McLaughlin, M. W., & Talbert, J. E. (1992, April). *Social constructions of students: Challenges to policy coherence.* Paper presented at the annual meeting of the American Educational Research Association, San Francisco.

Noddings, N. (1984). *Caring: A feminine approach to ethics and moral education.* Berkeley: University of California Press.

Oakes, J. (1985). *Keeping track: How schools structure inequality.* New Haven, CT: Yale University Press.

O'Neil, J. (1995). On schools as learning organizations: A conversation with Peter Senge. *Educational Leadership, 52*(7), 20-23.

Orr, D. (1994). *Earth in mind: On education, environment, and the human prospect.* Washington, DC: Island Press.

Poplin, M. (1993, April). *Voices from the inside.* Claremont, CA: Institute for Education in Transformation at the Claremont Graduate School.

Preston, J. (1991). *Gender and the formation of a women's profession: The case of public schoolteaching.* Working Papers Series, Wellesley College Center for Research on Women.

Rallis, S. (1989). Professional teachers and restructured schools: Leadership challenges. In B. Mitchell & L. Cunningham (Eds.), *Educational leadership and changing contexts of families, communities, and schools: Eighty-ninth yearbook of the National Society for the Study of Education* (pp. 184-209). Chicago: University of Chicago Press.

Regan, H. (1990). Not for women only: School administration as a feminist activity. *Teachers College Record, 91*(4), 565-577.

Richert, A. E. (1994, April). *The culture of inquiry and the challenge of change: Teacher learning and the school change context.* Paper presented at the Spencer Foundation Fellows Forum, New Orleans, LA.

Richert, A. E. (1995). *Stories that teach: Creating a context for teacher research on school change.* Unpublished manuscript.

Robertson, H-J. (1992). Teacher development and gender equity. In A. Hargreaves & M. Fullan (Eds.), *Understanding teacher development* (pp. 43-61). New York: Teachers College Press.

Rosenholz, S. (1989). *Teachers' workplace: The social organization of schools.* White Plains, NY: Longman.

Rossi, R. J., & Stringfield, S. C. (1995). What we must do for students placed at risk. *Phi Delta Kappan, 77*(1), 73-76.

Ryan, K. (1986). *The induction of new teachers.* Bloomington, IN: Phi Delta Kappa Educational Foundation.

Sacken, D. (1994). No more principals! *Phi Delta Kappan, 75*(9), 664-670.

Schein, E. H. (1992). *Organizational culture and leadership,* 2nd ed. San Francisco: Jossey-Bass.

Sarason, S. B. (1993). *The case for change: Rethinking the preparation of educators.* San Francisco: Jossey Bass.

Sarason, S. B. (1995). Some reactions to what we have learned. *Phi Delta Kappan, 77*(1), 84-85.

Schiraldi, V. (1995, December 1995). California builds more prisons than schools. *San Francisco Chronicle,* p. A6.

Schmuck, P., & Shubert, J. (1995). Women principals' views on sex equity: Exploring issues of integration and information. In D. Dunlap, & P. A. Schmuck (Eds.), *Women leading in education* (pp. 274-287). Albany: State University of New York Press.

Schön, D. A. (1983). *The reflective practitioner: How professionals think in action.* New York: Basic Books.

Schön, D. A. (1987). *Educating the reflective practitioner.* San Francisco: Jossey-Bass.

Senge, P. M. (1990). *The fifth discipline: The art and practice of the learning organization.* New York: Doubleday.

Sergiovanni, T. (1994). *Building community in schools.* San Francisco: Jossey-Bass.

Shedd, J. B., & Bacharach, S. B. (1991). *Tangled hierarchies: Teachers as professionals and the management of schools.* San Francisco: Jossey-Bass.

Soukhanov, A. H., & Severynse, M. (1992). *American heritage dictionary* (3rd ed.). Boston: Houghton Mifflin.

Sparks, D. (1995, Winter). A paradigm shift in staff development. *ERIC Review,* pp. 2-4.

Stodolsky, S. S. (1988). *The subject matters: Classroom activity in math and social studies.* Chicago: University of Chicago Press.

Strober, M., & Tyack, D. (1980, Spring). Why do women teach and men manage? A report of research on schools. *Signs, 5,* 494-503.

Sykes, G. (1996). Reform *of* and *as* professional development. *Phi Delta Kappan, 78,* 465-467.

Troen, V., & Boles, K. C. (1995). Leadership from the classroom: Women teachers as a key to school reform. In D. M. Dunlap & P. A. Schmuck (Eds.), *Women leading in education* (pp. 358-379). Albany: State University of New York Press.

Tuller, D. (1996, March 21). Californians' opinions of public schools plummets, poll shows. *San Francisco Chronicle,* p. B2.

Vygotsky, L. (1962). *Thought and language.* Boston: MIT Press.

Vygotsky, L. (1978). *Mind in society.* Cambridge, MA: Harvard University Press.

Wasley, P. A. (1993). *Teachers who lead: Rhetoric and reform and the realities of practice.* New York: Teachers College Press.

Watts, G., & Castle, S. (1993, December). The time dilemmas in school restructuring. *Phi Delta Kappan, 75*(4), 306-310.

Wehlage, G., Rutter, R., Smith, G., Lesko, N., & Fernandez, R. (1990). *Reducing the risk: Schools as communities of support.* Philadelphia: Falmer.

Weiss, C. H. (1993). Shared decision making about what? A comparison of schools with and without teacher participation. *Teachers College Record, 95*(1), 69-92.

Weiss, C. H. (1995). The four "I's" of school reform: How interests, ideology, information, and institution affect teachers and principals. *Harvard Educational Review, 65*(4), 571-592.

Wells, G., & Wells, G. (1992). *Constructing knowledge together: Classrooms as centers of inquiry and literacy.* Portsmouth, NH: Heinemann.

Wheatley, M. J. (1992). *Leadership and the new science.* San Francisco, CA: Berrett-Koehler.

Wheatley, M. J. (1995a). Leadership and the new science. In *Professional Development Briefs, 3,* 1-8. (Available from the Center for Ecoliteracy, 2522 San Pablo Blvd., Berkeley, CA 94702)

Wheatley, M. J. (1995b, February). *Whole systems change.* Presentation at the annual conference of the California Staff Development Council, San Francisco.

Wolf, K. (1991). The schoolteacher's portfolio: Issues in design, implementation, and evaluation. *Phi Delta Kappan, 73*(2), 129-136.

Zeichner, K., & Gore, J. (1989). *Teacher socialization.* East Lansing, MI: National Center for Research on Teacher Education.

Index